MW01129555

The Warriors
Part 2:
Imbeciles and Murderers

Norbert Aubrey

I

Copyright © 2021 by **Norbert Aubrey**

All rights reserved. No part of this publication may be reproduced, distributed or transmitted in any form or by any means, without prior written permission.

Ocean Ridge Press
Gualala, CA 95445
www.norbertaubrey.com

Publisher's Note: This is a work of fiction. Names, characters, places, and incidents are a product of the author's imagination. Locales and public names are sometimes used for atmospheric purposes. Any resemblance to actual people, living or dead, or to businesses, companies, events, institutions, or locales is completely coincidental.

The Warriors Part 2/ Norbert Aubrey -- 1st ed.
ISBN:978-1-7348-4303-3

Cover by Susan Bottorf,
 drawing by Felix O.C. Darley
courtesy of artvee.com

DEDICATION

Jamie and Sloane

Thanks to

John Bierhorst
Susan Bottorf
Nicole Stefanko
Leslie Hoppe
Laura Schatzberg
Margie Tygerson
Dan Wormhoudt

Congress's idea of strengthening the western district outposts with militia, once Congress had disbanded the Continental Army at the end of the Revolutionary War would *"defeat the purposes by their own imbecility"*
From a letter from soon to be Secretary of War Major General Henry Knox to retired General George Washington

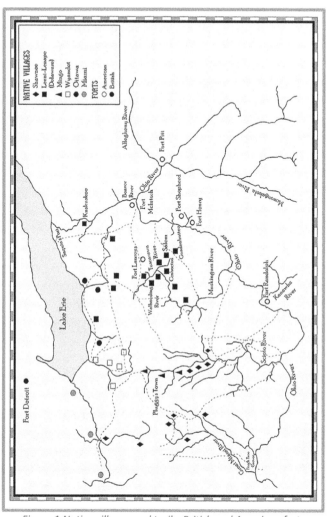

Figure 1 Native villages and trails; British and American forts

SCALPING

Scalping was first recorded by the Greek historian Herodotus in 440 BC. Scythian warriors presented the heads of their enemies to their kings and then removed the scalps to hang on the bridles of their horses.

The English were known to take the scalps of their enemies as early as 1043 AD. Although taking the heads as trophies was more common, scalps were easier to transport.

In America, before Europeans arrived, the natives scalped their enemies as proof they were dead. The taking of scalps of women and children was considered respectable because, to get one, a warrior had to enter enemy territory.

Europeans, however, were the first to consider bounties for scalps. The first recorded bounty offered in North America was by the Dutch governor of Manhattan in 1703, offering $60. During the French and Indian War, the governor of Massachusetts offered 40£ for males and 20£ for females and children. The Pennsylvania Governor offered 130 Spanish pieces of eight for males above twelve and 50 Spanish pieces of eight for females. The scalps were referred to as redskins. During the Revolutionary War, Lt. Governor Hamilton of British Canada was known by the settlers as the "hair-buyer general".

It was common in American history for both the natives and the European immigrants to scalp their enemies. The name "scalping knife" was a figment of

American and European writers' imagination. To the natives, a knife was a knife.

For more info:
  listverse.com
  newsmaven.io
  native-language.org

1 TURKEY

One day. just as the trees were starting to bud, Lewis Wetzel was visiting Bertha Rosencranz at her family's home. The log cabin sat on the hillside overlooking the Ohio River. He was sitting on a stump out in front while Bertha ran a comb through his hair. His long hair fell nearly to his waist.

"Gawd, I wish I had hair like yours, Lewis. It's so black and shiny."

Lewis was half asleep, enjoying the sun on his closed eyelids and the pleasure of the comb running through his hair.

Suddenly, a turkey gobbled. It seemed to be coming from across the river. Lewis stiffened and pushed her hand away.

"Aw, that's just an old Tom," Bertha said. "Wouldn't mind having him for dinner."

"No, it ain't," said Lewis. "Don't sound right."

"Sounds like every Tom turkey I ever heard," she replied. "What'dya think it is then? Sounds like one to me."

Lewis shrugged and relaxed back into her.

They watched as a man with a musket climbed into a canoe and paddled across the river.

"Ain't that Jason Wright?" Lewis asked.

"Poor fella. Ever since his missus died, he's been lonely. Maybe I'll go share that turkey with him, if you won't go get it for me," she pouted.

No one ever saw Jason Wright again. He'd often talked since his wife died of going downriver to

Kentucky, where the hunting was rumored to be better, so that's what people assumed happened to him. Or maybe he went to visit the ladies of the night hanging around Fort Pitt. No one paid much attention to his comings and goings. No one except Bertha and Lewis had seen him go, and what he did wasn't any business of theirs, and they had other things on their minds. They didn't give Jason Wright another thought.

When another turkey was heard gobbling the next day across the river and young Cornelius Cotton went to get his family some dinner and never returned, his family missed him. Everyone was suspicious. Maybe Lewis had been right.

Volunteers were called for, and twelve armed men crossed the river in three canoes. They searched up and down the riverside, but they couldn't find any sign of turkeys or Cornelius. They found his canoe, but there was no sign of him or Jason Wright. They tried to follow Cornelius' tracks, but they lost them in the thick underbrush.

A few days later, Lewis announced during dinner with Bertha's family that he was going to solve that mystery. That got her father and brothers laughing. They liked Lewis, mostly because Bertha liked him. They had heard the stories about Lewis coming back with two Indian scalps, but still, he was just a pimply-faced adolescent kid. He was boasting that he would solve a mystery that twelve grown men couldn't. They didn't know that Lewis had been exploring the Ohio country across from Wheeling at night. If they had known that, they would have thought him crazy.

Lewis was patient. He bided his time. He occasionally brought meat to the Rosencranz family, so they were always glad to have him over for dinner. In the evenings, he and Bertha would sit outside the cabin and talk. On those occasions, he would watch the river and the woods on the other side until the sun sunk behind the trees and it got so dark that he couldn't see anything on the other side. There were lots of bats at dusk. When it got dark, he could see the owls swooping down and hear the sounds of skunks and 'possoms and raccoons running through the leaves. Sometimes, it got downright noisy with crickets chirping, frogs croaking, fish splashing, and wolves howling.

One warm day in the late afternoon, he heard it, the call he had been waiting for: the turkey call. He didn't move, but all his senses snapped to high alert. He looked at every detail, every bush, every tree, and all the spaces between them until it got so dark he couldn't see anything but blackness. He listened, and he knew, he was certain, that it was too quiet.

That very night he snuck across the river, a mile upstream from Wheeling, in the Rosencranzs' canoe. He knew a few square miles of the land across the Ohio River as well as anybody on earth. He had been exploring it for months at night.

He landed the canoe and hid it in the brush. Then he quietly walked downriver, with his long rifle loaded. The turkey call had seemed to be coming from the foot of the hill. There was a cave in those hills facing Wheeling. He had discovered it one night when he ran through some bushes right into it. He had found himself inside a giant cavern. Lighting a torch of firebush, he had explored the cave. It wove underneath the hill for several hundred feet. There were old campfire rings inside and smoke stains on the ceiling and drawings on the walls, but it didn't look like it had been used for a long time. He had thought it an interesting curiosity because it was so well hidden from view, but the place gave him the creeps when the firebush burned out. He longed to show it to somebody, but nobody would cross the river with him. Even his pal Billy Boggs told him he was nuts to even consider it.

There was a good possibility that the cave was where the turkey call had come from. Lewis took his time getting to the top of the hill above the cave. It was pitch black, and he moved slower and made even less noise than a snail. Once on top above the cave opening, he sat with his back against a big oak. It was too dark to see the cave opening without the danger of slipping over the edge or making noise. Sunrise was a long way off. Without moving a muscle, he relaxed but stayed alert, listening and watching, with his loaded rifle lying across his thighs. He made himself stay awake. He promised himself he would sleep all day.

Eventually, the sky began to lighten. Lewis' eyes never left the bushes in front of the cave, twenty feet below. He heard some shuffling of feet, almost like a noisy mouse, and the hairs on his neck stood up. Time passed slowly. The rifle was heavy. His trigger finger was sweating. Vicious mosquitoes buzzed around him and feasted on his face and neck, but he didn't dare move.

Then, he heard the gobbling of a turkey. He leaned forward, just an inch to get a better look, with his finger on the trigger. He saw over the edge a bare-chested man, thin and dirty. He had moccasins on his feet. He was strutting back and forth, blowing on a whistle. His face was pockmarked. The only clothes he wore were a loincloth and leather leggings. His hair was just one sprout of greased black hair in a top knot sticking up from the back of his head. The morning light was shining on the man, and for a moment, Lewis was mesmerized.

Slowly lifting the rifle barrel, trying not to make any abrupt move that might attract attention, Lewis lay the cold barrel across his forearm, taking careful aim at the back of the man's head. His stomach knotted up. He remembered his vow as clearly as if he had just made it two years earlier when he was fourteen. 'From here on out, I aim to kill every injun that crosses my path, so help me God.' Everyone dismissed the vow then as the meaningless bluster of a kid as he gently squeezed the trigger.

Right before his eyes, the man's head disintegrated with the BOOM, and the body dropped to the ground. Lewis frantically reloaded as quick as he could, then waited for a long time, until the sun was nearly overhead, for anyone else to come out of the cave or for any sound at all. It remained eerily quiet. No one came out. Finally, he stood, stretched, and walked back down the hill to the side of the cave, crawling through the bushes close enough to see the cave entrance. Flies were already covering the bloody wound of the dead man.

He looked into the cave opening, rifle first, and when he confirmed it was indeed empty, he returned to the corpse, and, with the knife he always carried on his side, cut off the man's top-notch and the skin holding it. He removed the leather bag hanging from the man's neck, pulled off a silver bracelet from one of his arms, and sliced off a silver hoop nose-ring. He wiped the blade on the man's loincloth before returning to search the cave. There, he found a blanket, three muskets, and two pairs of boots.

He gathered up everything, returned to the canoe, and paddled with the current back across the river to Wheeling.

Word spread quickly that Lewis Wetzel had killed another Indian; the Indian that had taken Cornelius Cotton's life, and probably Jason Wright's, too, and he had the boots and muskets to prove it. For weeks afterwards, whenever he was around Wheeling, a crowd of children gathered around him just like they had done when he had killed the two horse thieves, begging him to tell the story of the Turkey Indian. Women smiled at him. Men tipped their hats. Everybody was frightened of the Indians, and now, here was somebody giving them hope and protection, something the army failed to do. The scrawny kid's reputation grew. He loved the attention.

2 TOMAHAWK

The Munsee Knotche was the acknowledged leader of the small warrior band. He led the Wyandot Goose and the Mingo Black Snake across the river at night with only one thing in mind: to avenge the death of two of their fellow warriors. They were going to kill the Wetzel boy. They knew where he lived. They had captured him on their first raid together.

It was a grim crossing. They had been fighting the Long Knives for three summers now and had little to show for their efforts, except the death of their friends. The Long Knives were even more numerous, and more were flooding down the river every spring and summer. On this trip, though, they weren't trying to persuade the immigrants to leave or steal horses and other valuables as "rent". They just wanted revenge by taking the scalp of the boy whose gun was always loaded. It was a dangerous crossing, as it always was, because they would be shot on sight. And they knew militia scouts would be watching the river.

"I still don't understand how he could have shot so many times," Black Snake said as he paddled from the bow of the bark canoe.

"He has supernatural powers," added Goose. "The Spirit favors him. We need to be very careful, or we'll meet the same fate as Otter and He Who Dances."

"The boy is very fast reloading, that's all it is," Knotche said as he steered the canoe. The stars were bright, but there was no moon yet. Wolves howled behind them, but it was eerily quiet on the Virginia shore. They could see a lantern at the Fort, but other than that, it was pitch black. *"We are three against one, and he is just a boy. We'll give him the justice he deserves."*

They paddled straight across and let the current take them downstream past Wheeling Creek. As they passed the eastern edge of the island, Knotche gave orders to paddle hard. The moon lit the way a few feet in front. Behind them, they could hear wolves howling. Ahead, they could see nothing. They were all silent, with the quiet tinkling of water off their paddles and the swishing of the canoe the only sound as they struggled sideways to the strong current until they slid into shore, scraping through a stand of young willows growing out into the river.

It took several hours to reach the Wetzel cabin. They had all been there before, when Heron was still alive, and the older Shawnee, Standing Tree, had given them confidence on their first raid. Now, there were only three in their original band. They avoided the cabins around Wheeling and headed up the same old Indian trail that met up with the creek as it looped down near the Ohio River. They didn't want any barking dogs to warn the soldiers of their presence. Once they were near the Wetzel cabin, they took turns sleeping so that one of them was on guard just in case of trouble.

They had agreed that they would use the same trick that had worked over and over for them on other raids. They would wait until the cabin door was opened in the morning, shoot whoever opened the door, then rush into the cabin and kill everyone in it, including the boy and all his relatives.

Everything went according to plan. They took turns standing guard. Knotche woke the other two at first light. They painted themselves to look as ferocious as possible, and then waited. And waited. The sun rose higher and higher, and nobody came out the door.

Goose finally said, *"This isn't right. This is making me nervous. I feel like we're the prey."*

"What do you suggest?" Knotche asked, irritated not only from the lack of sleep and the long trip to get there but that he'd put them all in danger, and it looked like it would be for nothing.

Black Snake said, *"Cover me."*

Before Knotche could stop him, he stood up and walked straight up to the cabin door. He knocked on the door with the bone handle of his knife.

The Wetzels had gone to church and a frolic afterwards for a cabin raising. It was late Sunday afternoon when the whole family rode up to the family cabin. George and Lewis rode out in front. Pa and Jacob brought up the rear. Everyone carried loaded muskets and rifles. They were jumpy because scouts had spotted Indians leaving the Virginia side of the river. They had already lost one member of the family. Martin hadn't been seen or heard from since the year before when he had answered the call from Morgan's Fort for someone experienced in Indian warfare.

Lewis was the first to see that they had had visitors. The door of the cabin was wide open. He slipped quickly off his mare and darted to the side of the cabin. George followed suit running to the other side. The others,

13

seeing their movements, turned their horses back and gathered up around Pa.

Lewis inched up to the front door, with his rifle in front of him and peered into the doorway. The cabin was mayhem. Clothes were scattered all over the floor, along with corn flour, grease, dried meat, and pots and pans. Sticking in the front of the door was a tomahawk.

George waved to the others that it was safe.

Lewis looked around the cabin and saw the moccasin prints. They had stepped in the flour. He followed them, crouching low, looking around uneasily, over to the barn. He found where they had been sleeping. He claimed he could smell them.

"You think it'll work?" Goose asked.

"You want to make a wager about it?" Black Snake said to Goose. *"I say that he can't resist. That boy loves Indian blood."*

"He can't miss our trail," Knotche stated. *"Any idiot could follow us, at least down to the river. We'll see him when he tries to cross. He'll be exposed. When he gets close to shore, we give him a little surprise. He won't be able to get away. It'll work. I'll bet on it."*

"Me, too," said Goose.

"Well, just for sport, I'm saying he doesn't come, although I think you're probably right," Black Snake replied. *"But you have to give me good odds."*

"I'll bet three buckskins against your one," said Goose.

"So will I," Knotche said."

Black Snake stuck out both hands, and they shook on it.

The three old friends sat in the shade of a big sycamore tree that leaned out over the river. The longer they waited, though, the more time passed without any sign of anybody. Lots of flies also shared the shade of the tree and were landing all over them, the men gently swatting them away.

Normally, story-telling was reserved for the winter, but to pass the time, Knotche said, *"These flies remind me of a story you'll like, Goose. My father told me this story."*

The two friends sat up and gave Knotche their attention.

"My story camps, called by name Wehixamukes (pronounced Way-he-kah- MOO-case). Wehixamukes agreed to watch a baby while the others were gone. He had been told when he nursed the baby, he must drive away the flies. The flies were just like this, and Wehixamukes got angry with the flies and said, 'I'm going to kill you.'

"He went and got his axe. When he came back to where the baby was sleeping, the flies were all over the baby's face. Well, Wehixamukes pulled back that axe and started chopping those flies all over the baby's face. Killed the baby."

Black Snake started laughing. Goose sat there horrified, with his eyes wide in disbelief.

"When he saw what he had done, he was scared. 'Now, what shall I do?' He said to himself. 'I've messed up!'"

"Yes, he did," added Goose.

Knotche continued. *"Then, he had an idea. He killed the goose who had been sitting on eggs under the cabin and stuck the feathers all over his body.*

"When the people came home, they asked, 'Where can the baby and Wehixamukes be?'

"They looked everywhere, and they found Wehixamukes under the house. A boy crawled under there, and there he was, sitting on the eggs. Wehixamukes made a loud noise 'SSSSS', just like a goose does to keep people away from her eggs, and there was Wehixamukes' butt sticking out of the feathers. Ihi!"

The story got Back Snake laughing and waving his butt at Goose, who himself sat there with eyes wide, not knowing if he should laugh or cry.

"What's taking that boy so long?" Goose asked.

What they hadn't counted on, what they didn't know, was that Lewis Wetzel did follow their trail, and he did see where they had crossed, and he was suspicious and careful.

Once reaching the river, Lewis found where the Indians had hidden their canoe. He sat at the edge of the river, looking across. Not only had the Indians not taken anything, but they had left a warning. He was on high alert when he saw that their tracks were so easy to follow. It was like they weren't even trying to get away. Ordinarily, he crossed the river at night. It was safer then. But, this time, he had a gut feeling that he shouldn't do it. And there was no compelling reason to, either. The Indians hadn't killed anyone nor stolen any horses. They had just made a big mess at his parents' cabin. And they had left a very nice tomahawk, one with a snake carved in its handle. He decided to let it pass.

3 MARTIN WETZEL

Previously, Martin Wetzel, Lewis's brother, and John Wolf had agreed to assist Colonel Zackquill Morgan as Indian experts in the attack against Pluggy's Town. They were on their way to Fort Morgan when they were spotted by a Shawnee patrol and were immediately attacked with musket fire. The shots missed both men. Wolf froze and raised his hands. He was immediately taken prisoner, and his hands were tied behind his back. Martin returned fire and took off running with five Shawnee warriors chasing him. He ran to the top of a hill and turned when the Indians fired at him. One bullet grazed his hip, another his shoulder. He stumbled but kept running. He crossed over the hill, ran to the bottom, and crossed over to the South Fork of Wheeling Creek.

Two more shots were fired at him, but they both missed. Martin, the adrenaline kicking in, took off running faster than he had ever run in his life in spite of his wounds. He didn't even notice the pain caused by the two bullets. The five Indians chasing him dropped their guns to make better speed. Martin ran down the creek through the thick brush, oblivious to the stickers and thorns and tree branches slapping his face and arms. On he dashed as fast as his legs could carry him. He knew his only chance was to get away. The water was shallow in the creek, and the bottom was gravelly and firm. He knew he could run fast. Whenever he entered a contest, he could usually outshoot and outrun the best of them. Only his younger brother Lewis was faster. As he ran, it began to dawn on him that he would get away. He was gaining ground.

Suddenly, he stumbled over a rock and went tumbling head over heels. Before he could get up, Standing Tree pounced on him, driving his knee into Martin's solar plexus. Martin saw the flash of a knife, and he struggled to block it, but the Indian had knocked the wind out of him when he landed on him. He couldn't catch his breath. He managed to grab Standing Tree's wrist and stopped the knife's point just under his chin. Four other Indians each grabbed one of Martin's limbs and held him down. He struggled to free himself.

The point of the knife cut into the loose flesh under his jaw. "No fight, you live," said the one on top of him.

Martin had no choice. He nodded and relaxed. They tied him up.

The Shawnee made camp that evening. Both Martin Wetzel and John Wolf were tied to small trees, but they couldn't see each other, and had no way of knowing what was happening to the other. They were a hundred yards apart in thick woods. Chief Black Hoof, the leader of the patrol, planned to kill them both, painfully.

Black Hoof ordered that dry wood be piled around the men. They would be burned where they were tied, as a lesson to all whites who dared enter Shawnee hunting land.

Wolf cried when he saw what they had in mind. Wetzel could hear him and tried to console him.

"Be a man, John. These are savages. Live a man, die a man. Go to heaven a man. They can't touch you," Martin called out.

Wolf only cried louder.

"Be strong, John," Martin yelled. "They can't hurt us. Not really."

But Wolf only cried louder.

Martin didn't see his friend anymore until John Wolf was nearly dead. He was too busy going through his own ordeal. At the small tree he was tied to, he didn't cry or beg. He glowered at his captors.

"Go ahead, you fucking savages. Burn me. I don't give a shit."

Standing Tree, the only one who understood more than just a few words of English, said, *"The white man says he doesn't care if we burn him."*

Black Hoof replied, *"Let's see. Line up for a little shooting practice."* The ten warriors grabbed their muskets and loaded them. They lined up in front of Martin.

Standing Tree stepped forward, with his back to Martin, facing the others. *"By rights, this prisoner belongs to me. I caught him."*

"We are not taking prisoners," Black Hoof replied. *"You may kill him if you want that honor."*

"This white has shown himself to be a brave man," Standing Tree replied. *"We are Shawnee. A brave man would be a welcome addition to our numbers."* Standing Tree looked at each man facing him with their muskets, one by one. It was not only praise for Martin but was an insult to them. The double meaning didn't escape them either, and they listened attentively. Oratory skill was respected by the Shawnee. Standing Tree had thought

that Martin looked familiar, too. He had wondered if this new captive was related by blood to the boys who had escaped from a multi-tribal raiding party he had joined two summers before. If he was, he was worth keeping, not killing. He'd already proven he was a fighter.

"I claim this prisoner, as is my right."

Black Hoof didn't answer right away but only looked at Standing Tree, then over at Martin. They talked. Standing Tree argued to spare Martin Wetzel's life. Martin couldn't understand a word of what was being said, but he knew they were talking about him. He glared at the chief.

"Let us see if this Long Knife is as brave as you believe," Black Hoof said. *"If he is, I agree with you. Another brave man added to our shrinking numbers would be good for our people, though this one has no manners. He calls us names and makes ugly faces. Look at him."*

The others looked and laughed at Black Hoof's joke.

"If he is a coward, we will treat him like the other one. Agreed?"

Standing Tree nodded. *"I will strike the fire myself."*

Black Hoof continued, speaking to all the warriors. *"I say, each of us takes a shot at this white man. A little game. We each try to get as close to him as possible without hitting him. We don't want to kill a brave man, if this Long Knife really is brave. If you are unsure of your aim or your musket does not shoot straight, then do not use a ball, but fire only powder. Get close."*

The warriors all murmured in approval, and Standing Tree stepped aside. Each of them stepped forward, one at a time, aimed, and fired. Some stood back. Others stepped up as close as a few feet. Martin scowled at each warrior, expecting each shot to be the end of his life on earth. The first ball went through his buckskin shirt and skinned his side. He winced in pain but didn't cry out. He wouldn't give them the satisfaction. He kept his head held high. Between each 'BOOM' of the muskets, he could hear, but not see, John Woods screaming and crying.

One shot, was aimed right at his heart. A young warrior, probably not older than fifteen, stood as close as any of them had come. He expected to die but stood up straighter and taller. The musket fired, the fire from the barrel scorched him, but nothing happened.

Shot after shot was fired. He could feel some of the balls whistle by his ears or feel the heat of them next to his shoulder. Another shot spun him around as a ball glanced off his hip bone. The rawhide knot tying him to the tree stopped him from being thrown off his feet. Eighteen shots in total were fired, and with each shot, Martin believed he was going to die. He had burn marks from the powder all over his chest and stomach and several flesh wounds where the bullets had nicked him.

Standing Tree untied him and walked him through the woods where a fire was burning around John Wolf. Wolf was writhing and squirming at his tree, and the flames burned his clothes. He was delirious. Shawnee warriors prodded him with spears and sliced open his belly, Wolf's intestines sizzled as they fell into the flames.

Days later, when Martin arrived at the Shawnee village along the Scioto River, he entered the village with a leather thong around his neck. His hands were tied behind his back. Crowds of children gathered around.

The village seemed to be waiting for him. Young warriors led him to a wigwam. It was a simple affair, like all the others. Twenty or thirty of them, rounded structures, five-foot-high covered with bark and sticks. The deerskin covering the doorway was pushed aside, and an elderly man, Chief Moluntha, stooped under the low doorway, stepped out, and stood up.

The Chief's hair was long and grey, and his face wrinkled. He had a large nose and a big forehead. One single eagle feather dangled from his hair, tied to a braid. There was a blue circular tattoo scrawled on both wrinkled brown cheeks. He was dressed like the warriors who brought him in. He wore just a loincloth and moccasins.

He looked Martin over. Martin ignored him, holding his head high, his chin slightly lifted, looking out over the shrunken old Chief towards the people gathering outside their homes. Moluntha pinched Martin's bicep, poked his finger into his stomach. There was no give. Martin was hard from living outdoors. Like his father, he was muscular, wider, and stouter than most of these Shawnee, who tended to be short and slim. The Chief walked around to look at Martin's back and poked his fingers into Martin's kidneys. He stuck his finger in the wounds, but Martin didn't give him the satisfaction of showing him it hurt. Moluntha walked back around.

Mouth." He indicated his own mouth. "Open."

Martin compliantly opened his mouth without changing his gaze.

"Good. Very good." The last time the old Chief had a white man brought to him, he'd burned him alive.

Moluntha nodded with his chin to a painted post forty yards away on a small knoll, on the far side of the village. The village was a big one by Shawnee standards. Besides the wigwams, the roof of a log house could be seen beyond the knoll. Martin could see that the post was painted yellow and blue and red with feathers and ribbons tied to it gently fluttering in the breeze. His stomach churned and tied itself in a knot. He knew they might kill him, but he had heard about the gauntlets. There was a chance that if he made it, he would live.

Between him and the pole, standing on both sides of the path they made, stood men, women, and children, all holding axes, sticks, clubs, and knives.

Standing Tree said to him," The Chief will protect you once you reach that pole."

"That's awfully kind of him," Martin said, sneering at Standing Tree.

I hope you make it. I do." Standing Tree looked at him kindly. His eyes were filled with sympathy. "Be bold and quick. Stay on the path. Try to run away, and you will die." Black Hoof, standing nearby, nodded.

Moluntha pointed at the rawhide ties and nodded with his chin to one of the young men. *"Untie the white man."* Martin's hands were untied.

Without a moment's hesitation, Martin took off, running towards the pole. Time itself shifted into a slower speed, and everything became more vivid. He took long strides and ran straight towards the first

24

man, a big man, bare-chested, who held a war club. Martin could see the snake carving highlighted on the handle, and he was surprised that he felt happy at its handiwork. His whole world became that first man. He saw that the man had yellow streaks across his cheeks and chest and the small bunch of his hair stood straight up like a tuff of grass. His forehead was sweaty, and there were lines of dirt in the creases. The man grimaced threateningly and then had to step back to avoid being run over by Martin. He raised the snake club to strike.

Martin suddenly changed directions, and the club swished through the air. He dodged, twirled, faked around the first group without being touched. In front of the long house, the people yelled and screamed and waved him forward, but they didn't close the path. They left it wide open for him to have room to run. He dashed straight down the middle, then abruptly weaved to one side, then the other, missing the swinging and plunging knives and tomahawks.

Suddenly, he was whacked on the back of the head as he twirled around, and he lost his balance in a sky of stars. He felt nothing. As he stumbled backwards, he saw a young woman with angry black eyes and long silky hair sneer at him with a self-satisfied triumph. He forced himself to spin forward, catching himself on a lanky teenager in the act of whipping a tomahawk down on him. Martin blocked the swing with his forearm and, with the other hand, snatched the tomahawk from the boy's grip and continued forward, rolling on the ground in a somersault, before scrambling to his feet. A woman jumped back, and Martin grabbed her knife and swung around, never stopping or slowing, letting both weapons draw a circle of safety. The people jumped back from him.

The path widened, and Martin raced for the pole.

Several young warriors, all holding tomahawks drawn back ready to swing, stepped into the path, blocking his way just in front of the pole. Rather than slowing, he sped up. They stood their ground and raised their tomahawks, but he dove to the ground and rolled through them like a log, knocking two of them over, and was back on his feet and grabbing the pole before they could respond.

True to his word, Moluntha protected Martin from further assault. The people dropped their weapons and crowded around to see up close this brave white warrior. Martin had passed their test.

That night, he was treated courteously and respectfully. The people sang and danced around the village campfire in front of the lodge house, entertaining him as a guest of honor. He was given choice cuts of raw buffalo liver. The Chief, in particular, showed him favor by offering to let Martin sleep in his wigwam with him and his two wives.

Later, a solemn ceremony was held, and Martin Wetzel was adopted into the family of Meadow Lark, who had lost her only son in Lord Dunmore's War. From that day forward, he was treated as a member of the tribe. And as each day passed, he was given more and more liberty.

4 RESCUE

The native tribes of the Ohio valley had agreed to stop fighting alongside the French in the French and Indian War when British officials agreed to remove their forts from Indian country. The British King also signed his Royal Proclamation banning settlements west of the Appalachian Mountains. When the British had not lived up to their promise to remove the forts, the Ottawa Chief Pontiac and the Mingo Half King Guyasuta had organized the various tribes. They burned down eight forts and scalped the soldiers as well as attacking settlements throughout the frontier. That war finally came to an end after a military stalemate resulted in negotiations.

Two years later, the British ally in those wars, the Iroquois Nation, a confederation of six tribes living in the east, in order to shift pressure from land jobbers away from their own land in New York, New Jersey, and Pennsylvania, sold land to the British across the Appalachian Mountains along the Ohio River in the western portions of Virginia which included present-day West Virginia and Kentucky. This was land the Iroquois had taken from the Hurons during the Beaver Wars a hundred years before. That sale took place at Fort Stanwix in New York.

The Lenape and the Shawnee lived on that land, but had not signed the treaty, nor had they even been allowed to participate in it. They had no intention of abiding by it, and attacks against settlers continued, which resulted in Lord Dunmore's War shortly before the Revolutionary War broke out. Lord Dunmore, Royal Governor of Virginia, organized the militia, who were objecting to the high taxes levied on them to pay for the French and Indian War and Pontiac's Rebellion. Lord Dunmore wanted the settlers to take out their animosity on the Indians instead of the British government. He led his army of militia volunteers to attack the Shawnee who were preventing settlement in the western portion of Virginia called Kentucky. Despite heavy losses, he forced the Shawnee Chief Cornstalk to sign a treaty relinquishing their Kentuck hunting grounds. The Shawnee were offered no compensation. It wasn't unusual for native tribes to sell land, but to do so took agreement from the entire tribe. Not even the major Chief of the tribe had that authority to give up their land and most of the Shawnee didn't feel bound by it.

At first, both the British and the Americans attempted to keep the Indians out of the Revolutionary War, but as the rebels proved more resilient than expected, the British began seeking Indian help and reinforced the idea that the settlers were trying to take the native land. When the Shawnee Chief Cornstalk presented himself to the Commander of Fort Randolph to talk peace after the Wyandot attack on Fort Henry, he was held prisoner and then murdered by militiamen. The Shawnee then joined the British and their western ally, the Wyandot. The Lenape, led by Chief White Eyes, turned down British appeals to ally with them and continued to stay out of the war. The British supplied guns and ammunition, and other supplies to all who would help the British cause. The raids on settlements continued, now with British-supplied weapons.

One summer day, scouts patrolling along the river spotted a band of Indians on the Virginia side of the river. The scouts tried to follow them without being seen but soon lost the trail. Captain Jed Morgan, the scouts' leader, sent a messenger back to Fort Henry warning of Indians in the vicinity and to be on guard. Colonel Shepherd sent out messengers to the stockades and blockhouses up and down the river. In turn, each refuge sent messengers farther out, trying to alert as many people as possible.

John Wetzel sent his sons out to warn those who hadn't yet forted up to come in where it was safe. George went south, Lewis went north.

Lewis had gone a few miles when he spotted a white man walking towards him under a heavy load. The man hadn't seen Lewis. Always up for a little fun, sixteen-year-old Lewis circled far around through the woods to intercept the man. He ducked behind a tree, hiding himself completely, and listened for the man's approach. He could hear the heavy boots shuffling along, getting closer and closer. Just as the man reached the spot where Lewis was hiding, Lewis jumped out in front of him.

"Boo!" Lewis yelled.

The man jumped a foot high and dropped his load. Meat spilled from a deer-skin onto the ground.

"Gol- darn!" he shouted. "You twattling groke! You scared me half to death!"

Lewis put his finger to his lips and whispered. "You ought to be. Walking along with injuns about like you was walking the streets around Fort Pitt. You're lucky I ain't no injun, or you'd have lost your scalp."

"Indians? It's not safe here?" He glanced all around.

"Nope," Lewis replied.

"But this is our land. The Indians live across the river."

"Tell that to them varmints. They're here. Now."

Lewis introduced himself and told of his errand. Frazier Reynold was a young man of twenty and new to the area. They shook hands. Lewis helped him bundle back up his load, and they headed down the trail together. A passing rain shower drenched them both.

"Might as well wash my hair!" Lewis said. He undid the bun in his hair and let the hair fall down his back. The long black hair fell all the way down his back.

Frazier was a newcomer to the area, from Pennsylvania. While they walked along, he told Lewis his story. Lewis listened half-heartedly, but most of his attention was on the trail ahead and the woods on both sides. He was a little irritated to not be running, but he didn't want to be anti-social and leave the man alone. The fool could get himself killed. His eyes shifted all around, never staying in one spot. He listened for any sounds at all, and even if a bird chirped or a squirrel dropped a nut, Lewis wasn't satisfied until he knew what it was. His nose was active, too, sniffing for anything out of the ordinary.

Frazier told Lewis he had just been married a month before after getting his girlfriend's father's permission to start a life together. Rose was now waiting for him at their cabin while he went to get food. He'd had a hard time finding anything and had gone farther than he'd expected.

"I saw lots of deer last evening. I should have popped one when I had the chance."

Lewis just said, "Yep."

Frazier couldn't stop talking about his wife. He looked off into the sky, where he could see her in his mind's eye. "Rose is the most beautiful woman you ever saw. Wait till you see her. Long red hair. She's Irish, you know? Rosy cheeks. Teeth like pearls. And you should see her figure." Frazier whistled. "She's a looker, that's for sure, but that isn't all. Rose is a wonderful cook. You'll have to stay a while and have her cook you up a venison steak. You'll see."

"Can't. Maybe another time." Lewis' eyes never left the woods around them.

By the time they neared Reynold's cabin, they had been walking together for a half-hour. Lewis remarked that he smelled smoke when they were still a good ways off.

"She's probably got a good fire going. She's a remarkable woman. Always thinking ahead."

Lewis grabbed Frazier by the arm and pulled him off the trail. He pointed up to the sky ahead. There were thin wisps of smoke.

"What?" asked Frazier.

"That ain't no cook-fire," Lewis said. He glanced all around uneasily.

"Oh, sure it is," said Frazier. "What else could it be?"

"Injuns," said Lewis.

"Naw. I was just there. Rose is fine. She wasn't even out of bed yet when I left. Besides, injuns wouldn't bother her. She treats them like family. She respects them."

"Shut up." Lewis peered around the tree, glancing all around. "Leave the meat. Load your gun," he ordered.

Frazier obediently did what he was told. He was suddenly nervous and glanced around behind him.

"When I run to that yonder tree," Lewis pointed to a big oak farther down the trail, "you keep your eyes open. If anything moves, shoot it. Got that?"

Frazier nodded. His eyes were wide, and he was turning pale.

"And breathe!"

Lewis took off like a jackrabbit, darting back and forth at full speed, with his knees high, until he reached the big oak. Then, he turned and waved for Frazier to come. Frazier ran, zigzagging like Lewis had done.

They kept getting closer and closer to the cabin until they saw the smoldering ruins. Smoke was drifting up from red coals.

"That's my cabin!" cried Frazier. "Rose! Rose!" He called out. He dropped his gun and started towards what was left of his cabin. Lewis grabbed his arm and pulled him back.

"Careful," he warned. "Ain't no use losing your scalp."

Frazier nodded. Together, they crept through the woods until they reached the clearing where the cabin had stood. Lewis looked all around, studying each bush and tree all around the perimeter. There was no sound except an occasional crackle from the coals. Nothing moved. Lewis finally decided it was clear and walked to the smoking ruins. Frazier ran around calling out for Rose. Lewis studied the ground.

"Rose! Darling! Where are you? It's safe now! Rose! I'm here!"

"She's alive," Lewis said, pointing to the ground. "There's four of them varmints who took her. They went this-a-way."

Frazier looked at the jumbled footprints in the muddy soil. "Oh, Gawd!" he cried. He sank to the ground. "Oh! I never expected this! Oh, Rose! I'm so sorry, Rose! What am I going to do?" He bawled.

"Get up. Let's go get her," Lewis said quietly. "Are you game?"

Frazier looked up, wiping the tears with the back of his hand. "There's too many."

"There's a bunch of them varmints, sure enough," Lewis said matter-of-factly.

"This isn't your fight," Frazier announced. "I can't expect you to risk your neck for my problem. Hell, we're almost strangers."

"I ain't got nothing better to do," Lewis smiled. His face lit up. "C'mon, time's a-wasting. They ain't far ahead."

Lewis followed the trail into the woods. The Indians' trail was hard to follow because the Indians stepped carefully into each other's footprints. But, occasionally, he spotted the print of a bare foot, which helped. Lewis guessed that was the woman's. The Indians and their captive also walked across logs and rocks when they were available. But Lewis could see that the trail led towards the river. They lost it completely for a while. They circled around in ever-widening circles and picked up the trail again, and followed it all the way to the river bank.

Poking around in the willows, Lewis found some of the leaves were turned the wrong way. He waded into the river and looked closely at the muddy bottom. The water was clear, and he spotted a faint yard-long indentation. Frazier stood on the bank watching Lewis. Lewis pointed at the mark in the mud. "There! They had a canoe. This is where they crossed."

Frazier looked, but he couldn't see what Lewis was pointing at.

"Now, what do we do?" Frazier asked. "We can't cross the river. And even if we did, it's too dangerous there. Those Indians'll kill us. Even I know that."

"You want to give up?" Lewis asked. He looked up at the man innocently.

"Well, no. I mean I have to save Rose or die trying. But I can't ask you to risk your life."

"You don't need to. I'm going across whether you're coming or not. You coming?"

Frazier nodded.

"Good. Grab every piece of driftwood you can find. Big stuff. And be quick about it." Lewis himself started wading along the shoreline, grabbing pieces of floating wood stuck in the willows and flinging them ashore. Frazier did the same. Then Lewis pulled out his tomahawk and started chopping long pieces of wild grapevines growing among the trees. Together, the two of them built a small raft.

"Can you swim?" Lewis asked.

"Yes."

"Good. Do as I do." Lewis stripped off his clothes and wrapped his rifle, powder horn, bullet pouch, knife, tomahawk, and moccasins in his deerskin trousers, wrapped it all in his hunting shirt, and set the bundle in the middle of the raft. Frazier did the same. Together, they pushed the raft away towards the opposite shore. They held onto the raft and kicked. The current was moving slowly to the west, and it carried them downriver, but it wasn't long before they were on the opposite shore. Lewis yanked on his clothes and was off looking for the Indians' landing spot while Frazier tied his boots.

Lewis spotted the Indians' canoe. They hadn't been as careful on the other side of the river. Rather than sink it in the water, they had pulled it up on shore and covered it with branches.

He found a crushed plant and then a footprint. He hurried along with Frazier right behind him. "They may be taking their time, now that they think they're safe," Lewis whispered. "If we hurry, maybe we can catch them before dark. But we have to be quiet, too."

Frazier nodded. He looked up. The tree canopy was thick, and he couldn't see much blue sky, but the sunlight was already coming from the west. Lewis started running down the trail, Frazier following him. It rained, but they kept going.

The trail wasn't hard to follow until the light started to fade. Then they had to slow down, and Lewis was sniffing his way and even got down on his hands and knees occasionally to see if he could find footprints.

When it turned fully dark, they were both ready to give up the chase for the night and resume in the morning when Lewis said, "Smell that?"

"What?"

"Fire." Lewis put his finger to his lips. He loaded his long rifle, Frazier doing the same. They started walking slowly ahead in the dark. They hadn't gone far when they spotted the light of a fire flickering through the brush. It was farther away and more difficult to get to, though, than just walking in a straight line. It was on another hilltop to the west. They worked their way slowly down the hill they were on. They lost sight of the fire. At the bottom, there was a swampy stream and brambles. They carefully picked their way through the thick brush before starting up the hill on the other side. As soon as Lewis spotted the fire again, he lay down on his stomach. Frazier did the same.

The two crawled their way closer and closer, like two snakes. The damp leaves from the rain earlier in the day kept the leaves from rustling as they slithered their way closer.

At the campsite, they spotted Rose first. She was huddled against a tree, softly sobbing. Three lumps were lying around the fire, asleep. A fourth man was sitting with his back against a tree. They could see his topnotch. His bare chest glistened in the firelight. He was staring into the fire.

Lewis signaled for Frazier to back up. Frazier shook his head no. He was suddenly filled with rage. He wanted to rush the camp right now and get his Rose back.

Lewis pushed himself back next to Frazier. He held his finger to his lips. He pointed back the way they'd come and then moved his fingers like a bird talking.

Frazier reluctantly nodded and followed Lewis back down the hillside, back across the swamp, and then up the other side to the hill they'd started on.

When they were far enough way, Lewis said softly, "Let's talk."

"Why didn't we save her? We could get them, Lewis," Frazier pleaded. "Please! We have to save my Rose! We could charge them with guns a-blazing and grab her and be off. Please help me."

"They'll kill her. That's what them varmints do, first thing when they're attacked. They kill the prisoners. We wait till dawn. Less chance of them killing her if we get them when they're first waking up."

"You sound like you've done this before."

Lewis nodded.

The two bedded down next to each other, covering themselves with drier leaves they found underneath a big maple. Frazier couldn't sleep at all but lay there going over and over in his mind what he would do to save his wife in the morning. Lewis was sound asleep in minutes with his rifle lying at his side.

An owl woke Lewis up, and he instinctively grabbed his rifle. He lay there for a few minutes, then roused Frazier.

"Time to go fetch your missus," Lewis whispered.

They crept back over to the Indians' camp. On the way, Lewis explained his strategy. They would wait until the first of the Indians began to wake up. They would shoot the first two to get to their feet. Lewis would take whoever was on the left, Frazier would take whoever was on the right.

"What happens if only one gets up, or three?" Frazier asked.

"If it's one, I'll take him, and you shoot the guard." If it's more than two, same as two. You shoot the man on the right. As soon as you shoot, yell as loud as you can, "Get em, boys!" and charge them with your knife. Got it?" Frazier looked at Lewis wide-eyed, then nodded.

When they crawled up to within sight of the Indians' camp, a different guard was leaning against the tree. It was a white man with a beard. Three men were asleep next to the still glowing embers of the fire. Rose, too, was sprawled on the ground.

Lewis' and Frazier's rifles were loaded and ready. Slowly, the surroundings came into clearer and clearer focus as it got lighter. Birds started chirping and flying around. The guard, the bearded white man, walked over to the fire pit and picked up a pile of sticks and leaves and noisily tossed them on the fire.

"You'd sleep all day if I'd let ya," the man grumbled. "Come on, rise, and shine." He nudged each of them with his boot.

One of the Indians yawned and stretched. Another rolled over away from the fire. The third pushed the boot away. Rose looked up.

Just as the first Indian stood up, Lewis whispered, "Now!"

An explosion of sound roared through the quiet morning as the two rifles fired. The guard fell into the fire with a bullet in his forehead. An Indian went flying backwards with a bullet in his chest.

Both Lewis and Frazier leaped up, yelling, "Get 'em, boys!" Lewis was already swinging his tomahawk at one Indian's head as the man tried to stand. The other rolled away from Frazier, leaped up, and ran into the woods with Frazier right behind him. Lewis scooped up Rose, tossed her over his shoulder like a sack of potatoes, and ran back down into the gully. There was a thick pawpaw patch there. He set her down, holding his finger to his lips for silence. "Crawl in there, ma'am. Don't come out until I call you."

She nodded, wide-eyed.

Lewis ran back up the hill, loading as he ran, and took off running the way he'd seen Frazier and the Indian go. He hadn't gone far before he came across the two, facing each other, circling around, each holding a knife. They were bloody from slashes across both their chests.

Lewis calmly set on one knee, took quick aim, and shot the Indian.

"I had him, Lewis. Dammit."

Lewis just shrugged. "You can have him now. Take his scalp."

Rose was still hiding in the pawpaw patch when the two men walked down into the gully loaded down with four scalps, knives, tomahawks, guns, and jewelry taken from the Indians.

"You can come out now, ma'am," Lewis said.

Rose crawled out. She burst into tears when she saw Frazier, and wrapped her arms around him and covered him with kisses. She tried to hug Lewis, too, but he squirmed away from her.

"That ain't necessary, ma'am. Best we get out of here.

5 SIGNING UP

A private nailed the notice to the inside of Fort Henry's front gate, and a crowd gathered around. John Wetzel and his sons, George and Lewis, looked at the notice, but only George could read English. Pa could read only German. Lewis was illiterate.

"What's it say?" asked Lewis.

"Says that the new Commander at Fort Pitt is looking for volunteers for three-month enlistments. You'll be home by Christmas. And listen to this! Paying almost seven dollars a month! Heck, that's more than double what they normally pay! They'll be taking sign-ups here in the courtyard at noon today."

Lewis looked up at the sky. It was nearly noon now. "I'd like to kill me some more injuns," he said. His desire to kill as many Indians as he could was as strong now as the day he'd made his oath.

"What'll you do with twenty dollars?" George asked.

"I'd have me a good time."

Pa cuffed him on the back of the head. "I can't tell you how to live, Lewis. You're almost a man. But your Ma would have a fit, her boy getting himself killed running off with the army. Besides, you ain't old enough. You can get that idea out of your head right now, boy!"

"Aw, Pa. I'm old enough to kill injuns. Ain't no age limit on that."

"Sir," said George. "He is, too, old enough. Says here sixteen to sixty."

"Then you're a dang fool if you go off with the army," Pa declared. "Army ain't nothing but trouble. 'Do this, do that. Go here, go there.'"

"Well, I'm a man, and you can't stop me," Lewis announced.

Pa just shrugged and mumbled, "Yeah, sure you are," and walked out the gate and down to the river to check on his catfish lines. George ran to catch up with him.

Two recruiters from Fort Pitt took seats on upended logs at a wooden table, one with a sheet of parchment to take the names of volunteers, the other giving instructions to each recruit. Lewis and his pal Billy Boggs stood in line behind several other volunteers. Billy had a silky, wispy start of a mustache and curly brown hair. He was short with broad shoulders. Lewis was string bean skinny, with a face marked by smallpox scars. His black hair fell almost to the back of his knees. He had wide shoulders on his bony frame. Billy signed his name with a flourish on the line, and the recruiter looked at his name with no questions asked. Before Lewis could sign his X, the recruiter asked, "You sixteen? You got to be sixteen to go on this expedition."

Lewis had turned sixteen the month before, in August. Billy was a couple of months older but looked older now that he had facial hair. Lewis and Billy looked at each other, and Lewis spoke up first, but his face flushed red, and his adolescent voice shifted back and forth from low to high like a frog to a bird. "Yes sir, I'm sixteen. Ain't I Billy?"

"Yep, he is," said Billy.

"What's your name, son?"

"Lewis. Lewis Wetzel."

"You Captain Wetzel's boy?"

"Yes, sir."

"He know you're volunteering?"

"Yep. He don't care."

"Then go get your Pa to vouch for your age. Next."

Lewis turned away crestfallen.

"You supply your own gun and ammunition. Muster when you hear the bugle in the morning. Understood?" Billy nodded.

Lewis caught up with his father before he and George reached the river.

"Sir, I need you to vouch for me with the recruiter."

John Wetzel looked his son over, head to toe. He looked back towards the fort. "What for?"

"He don't believe I'm sixteen."

Pa was conflicted. He was glad the new Commander at Fort Pitt, General McIntosh, was going to do something about the Indian threat. The previous general hadn't done anything except muck things up. And he was glad the Wetzels wanted to do their share. He was proud that his boy wanted to go after the Indians, though his wife wouldn't like it. But he was worried about him, too. He knew Lewis could take care of himself. He'd proven that. Lewis had grown up around the Indian threat, and he had taught Lewis everything he possibly could to be well prepared. But he knew anything could happen on those army expeditions.

"You go ahead, George. I'll catch up with you in a few minutes." Pa turned back towards the fort with his hand on Lewis' shoulder. "Well, son," Pa said, walking back up the hill, "I want you to be careful. Being with the army isn't like running around in the woods by yourself. Every injun within a hundred miles will know you're there, and they'll want to take potshots at you, too. Just remember the rules."

"I know Pa. Keep my eyes open, my mouth shut, and never volunteer."

"You're a good boy, Lewis. You always paid attention to your old Pappy." Pa slapped him on the back.

Pa signed his name right next to Lewis' X to verify that he had his approval to go on the expedition.

6 THE ARMY

Lewis and Billy mustered with the other militiamen. The volunteers made their way upriver on flatboats. Both boys had rifles with them, but not everybody did. They were assigned to Company 3 with other men from Virginia. A middle-aged man, Amos Porter, was voted company commander, though neither boy knew him. He was elected because he was friendly and told good jokes.

Once at Fort Pitt, they set off the very next morning. Captain Porter tried to get them to march along like the Continentals. They tried, but none of them had any practice marching and soon lost interest. Mostly everybody thought it was stupid and ignored Porter's orders to stay in line. After marching for an hour, the sun starting heating up, and men from other companies kept stopping along the trail, taking a break under shady trees. Their Captains were kept busy moving them along.

Lewis stayed alert as was his way, peering into the woods and listening as they walked along, but it didn't take him long to understand why his Pa didn't liked the army. They were noisy. Any attacker could hear them coming from a mile away, and they were easy targets.

"You getting hungry?" Billy asked.

"Yep."

"Hey, Captain! When are we stopping for some lunch?" Billy called out.

"We just had breakfast!" the Captain replied.

"But I 'm hungry," Billy said.

Lewis glanced up at the sun but didn't say anything. He didn't much care for this walking along with a bunch of other guys into Indian land, led by a "friendly" Indian. He didn't care what Chief White Eyes' role was. He was still an Indian, and he hated all Indians. Everybody always said you can't trust them, and he didn't.

Chief White Eyes, sometimes called Grey Eyes, for his startlingly grayish eyes highlighted by wire-rim glasses, was a simple, honest man. He supported and approved of the Moravian Christian influence on his tribe, although he was not a Christian. He was the head civil chief of the Lenape, the tribe the Americans called Delaware. Civil chief meant that he was in charge of the tribal affairs in time of peace. The Lenape were thought by the other tribes to have the wisest leaders in the Ohio Valley, a tribe that was revered by many other tribes as their Grandfather. White Eyes' hair was long with a touch of grey, and he dressed simply in plain moccasins, linsey-woolsey trousers, and a linen shirt. He was married to a white woman who had been kidnapped when she was five years old and raised by the Lenape. They had one young son.

Chief White Eyes had offered to personally lead the army across Lenape land and point out possible building sites for forts to the new Commandant of the Western District, General Lachlan McIntosh, a Scotsman from Georgia. Washington had recommended McIntosh for the job after getting to know him at Valley Forge, where he'd been transferred after killing Georgia Congressman Button Gwinnet in a duel.

The first action General McIntosh had taken when he relieved General Edward Hand of command of the Western District was to conduct the Fort Pitt Treaty with the Delaware, something General Hand had already arranged, in order to obtain permission to cross their land. With Washington's approval and the Lenape's agreement, McIntosh had a different objective than his predecessor. He planned to build a series of forts across Lenape territory closer and closer to the British at Fort Detroit. The best way of protecting the people living on the western frontier, it was generally believed, was to get rid of the British influence on the Indians.

Chief White Eyes and war chief Hopocan had both signed the Fort Pitt Treaty after McIntosh agreed to White Eyes' request to establish a fourteenth Indian state, added to the thirteen rebelling United States, a state in which the Lenape and any other tribe who wished to participate could join in. McIntosh assured White Eyes that it wasn't up to him, but he would encourage the Continental Congress to adopt that measure and told the Lenape leaders he was confident Congress would. White Eyes was so convinced it would be a reality and was so happy with that prospect that he agreed to lead the army himself to suitable building sites.

McIntosh also agreed to Chief Hopocan's demand that a trading fort be built close enough to their villages so that the Delaware could not only trade their furs for the modern supplies his people needed but also would provide protection from the British and their Indian allies. The Lenape would need that fort and the protection of its guns and soldiers if they actively assisted the Americans.

As the army marched along following Chief White Eyes, another hour passed as the men dropped off here and there in twos and threes. Those who had brought along food stopped to have a bite to eat or take a nap.

Billy called out again. "Hey, Captain! I'm hungry. I thought the army was feeding us." Other men started grumbling, too. Many of the Virginia militiamen had traveled long distances to the muster and didn't have extra food like the men who lived closer to Fort Pitt.

"OK, OK, hold your horses, Private Boggs. I'll check on it." Captain Porter jogged on ahead to catch up with the Continentals leading the way behind Chief White Eyes.

He was back in a half-hour. "Listen up, men of Company 3," he called out as they walked along, straggling, in small groups. "We're making camp for lunch in another mile. I'm going to need some volunteers to collect firewood once we get there, and somebody to help set up the command tents. If you don't volunteer, you'll get selected for latrine duty."

The pace picked up. "What about it, Boggs? Firewood?" the Captain asked.

"Sure."

"Wetzel?" Lewis shook his head no, remembering his father's advice about volunteering.

"Tents, then?"

Again, Lewis shook his head.

"OK, then you've got latrine duty."

Lewis nodded. He didn't know what latrine duty was.

The Captain went down the line giving assignments.

That's when the grumbling started. It had been a long morning walk, and all the men were hungry, but the army didn't have sufficient supplies to feed full rations until the cattle arrived that had been requisitioned for this expedition. General McIntosh had stayed behind to inquire about them and other requisitions, too, and was still waiting for their arrival at Fort Pitt. The officers were expecting the Lenape to start supplying them food, something Chief White Eyes, and Chief Hopocan had agreed to do, misunderstanding the translation during the Treaty negotiations. They had thought they were agreeing to feed a friend if he were hungry, not feed a traveling army.

Food was in short supply, though their destination was a mere twenty-five miles downriver from Fort Pitt. At first, the men were allowed to hunt if they spotted a deer or an elk or a bear. But when soldiers went off hunting and didn't come back, Colonel Brodhead, the Continental officer in charge, ordered that only four men could leave at one time. The militiamen ignored the order. Others merely drifted into the woods and circled back home. Food wasn't all that was in short supply. The Quartermaster was ordered to distribute awls and thread so that the soldiers could repair their clothing and make moccasins if they bagged a deer.

Arguments broke out between the units, especially between the Pennsylvania and Virginia men. The officers had to intervene. They ordered that the non-commissioned officers were not allowed to barter meat or skins to another regiment, though they could give or sell it to their own.

When the Continental officers called a halt for lunch, the men separated into units. The Continentals from Virginia set up camp next to the river. The Pennsylvania Continentals set up in the woods. The only militia companies were from Virginia. No Pennsylvania militia were along on this expedition, although it was confusing and not a clear-cut difference because both Pennsylvania and Virginia claimed the same land around Fort Pitt, so nobody was sure which state they were from. The so-called Pennsylvania militia were supposed to come later with General McIntosh. The militiamen stopped along the river near the Virginia Continentals.

The camp wagons and followers set up in the middle of the trail. Rations were distributed by the order of Colonel Gibson of the Virginia Continentals. Half rations.

Problems escalated when one of the Virginia Continentals called over to the Pennsylvania camp, "You lollipops is licked!"

"Cram it, you country bumpkin," was the reply from the Pennsylvania camp.

"You're a bunch of cock robins," a Virginia militiaman called out, referring to the Pennsylvania Continentals.

"You hillbillies enjoying your fire-cake?" Came the reply. That's what most of them were eating except the friends of the one man who had managed to bag a deer or the militiamen who had the money to buy something from the camp-followers. Fire-cakes were a half ration of flour mixed with water cooked over a fire.

Lewis didn't plan to eat fire-cakes for lunch, nor did many of the other militiamen, and he snuck off to catch himself something else. But there were so many people running around in the woods, and the camp was so noisy that there was no game to be found. Luckily, his Ma had packed him a fish-hook and a length of line, and he managed to catch a catfish on a piece of fire-cake. It was big enough to feed him and Billy. He loaned the hook out to another man, who also caught a catfish.

As a prank, Billy dared Lewis to deposit the fish guts without getting caught over in the Pennsylvania camp when they stopped for the night. Lewis took up the challenge. He carried the guts wrapped in some leaves when the march started again in the afternoon.

When they camped for the night, Lewis slipped the fish guts next to the Pennsylvania command tent before turning in.

Lewis was assigned the four am to six am watch. He didn't mind it at all, although it was a difficult watch because those standing that watch had to wake up and then stay wide awake while everyone else was snoring away. It was getting cool, too, which made it hard to stay awake. That was his favorite time, though, when he could be alone and soak in the looks, sounds, and smells of the ancient forest. He yearned to go running around and look things over, but he was threatened with one-hundred lashings if he left his post.

During Lewis' watch, he heard a clamor coming from the Pennsylvania camp and several gunshots. He shot, too, thinking they were under Indian attack. He shot high because he couldn't see anybody and didn't want to hit one of his own. He ducked behind a tree with his rifle and reloaded as fast as he could.

It turned out that a bear was attracted to the smell of the fish guts. The prank backfired because the Pennsylvania Line had bear meat for breakfast. They wouldn't share.

The name-calling continued. Not all the Virginia militiamen were from Virginia. The ones living near Fort Pitt considered themselves Pennsylvanians. The Continentals from the Virginia Line didn't care for their own militiamen, considering them untrained and untrustworthy. Fistfights broke out, and the Continental officers lectured the militia commanders to control their men, but that was asking of them something they had no power to do.

The next day, with everyone except the Pennsylvania Continentals hungry, men continued slipping off into the woods to hunt. Others slipped away with no intention of coming back. Colonel Gibson, second in command, was forced to ban the practice, but after much persuasion by the militia commanders, who pointed out that there wasn't enough to eat, he relented and allowed two men at a time from each unit to go on hunting duty. The hunting continued to be poor.

Lewis didn't like somebody telling him what to do and when to do it. When to get up, when to go to bed, but peeing and shitting in a hole in the ground that he had to dig because the army directed him to, was too much, and he relieved himself whenever and wherever he wanted to, like most of the militiamen.

Few of the soldiers - both the Continentals and the militiamen - liked being led by an Indian, and many were convinced Chief White Eyes was leading them into a trap. They proceeded uneasily, expecting the Indians to attack them at every narrow section of the trail or from behind every bush. The militiamen fired their guns at all hours of the day and night at every moving bush and every owl, hawk, or crow.

The Pennsylvania Continentals bickered with the Virginians. The Continentals from Pennsylvania came from an area that tried to cooperate with the Indians in the fur trade. There had been mostly peace for many years between the whites and Indians when nearly all the whites were Quakers. The Indian fur trade was their bread and butter. The Seneca and Wyandot kept attacking them, but they would usually leave the Quakers alone. The Pennsylvanians believed the British were behind the Seneca attacks because the British traders wanted the fur trade to themselves.

The Virginians, both Continentals and militiamen, didn't want to cooperate with Indians. They saw them as unreasonable savages who attacked their settlements without cause, encouraged by the British. They built their homes on land that they had legally acquired, but the Indians claimed that land belonged to them.

Overall, it was an unhappy army marching down the trail, following an Indian through the wilderness.

To make matters worse, the militiamen wouldn't obey the commands of the Continental officers, and often their own elected officers, either. They rested whenever they felt like it and when ordered to get up and march, even the militia officers thumbed their noses at the Continentals.

Chief White Eyes was uneasy with the behavior of all the soldiers. They were uncouth in actions and appearance. They were loud and disrespectful and shot at every animal they saw, and when they killed something, they failed to offer up tobacco or give any thanks at all. He wasn't comfortable with them. Most of the whites that he knew, the missionaries, and Colonel Morgan, the Indian Superintendent, weren't like this at all. Lenape warriors would never act this way. They had manners.

When the army stopped on the second night, Lewis went out to check out the lay of the land. Tents were set up, firewood gathered. Chief White Eyes watched with curiosity as the white soldiers chopped down trees with axes. Green wood wouldn't burn. Why would they do that? He wondered why they didn't just pick up dead wood that was lying all around.

He noticed Billy Boggs carving his initials in a big oak and walked up to him. He held out his hand. "How d'ye do?" He knew a few words, but it was the only English phrase he knew. Billy Boggs looked at the outstretched hand. "Pleased to meet ya, Chief," Billy said and continued to carve his initials.

"B. B. That's me," Billy said, proud of his handiwork. He was halfway through the second letter.

White Eyes said in Algonquin. "*This is Lenape land, and you are guests here. You should respect this tree.*"

Billy looked up at the Chief. "Huh?"

A man nearby said. "He says he'll rent us his daughter for a flip-penny."

"I wish," Billy laughed.

Chief White Eyes frowned when Billy continued carving. He used one of the few English words he knew. "No!" He slapped his hand over the carving.

"I guess he wants more than a penny," Billy laughed. But he got the message.

7 THE FORT

The financial situation hadn't improved back at Fort Pitt with the arrival of General McIntosh, and the troops were not happy. Desertions were frequent, drunkenness was common, as was thievery and neglect of duty. A local farmer complained to Colonel William Crawford, McIntosh's second in command, that soldiers had killed his pigs. McIntosh was anxious to get his soldiers and the militiamen, who had short term enlistments, away from the settlement around Fort Pitt. Once out into the wilderness, he expected the clamoring for pay, the drunkenness, and desertions to stop.

The major problem he was trying to resolve was the same as General George Washington encountered, too, in Valley Forge. The Continental Congress had no way to raise funds, so they had to appeal to the states to provide for the army. But the citizens of Virginia and Pennsylvania didn't want to pay more taxes to fund McIntosh's army. One of the major reasons they were rebelling against the British in the first place was because of the high taxes Parliament had been trying to impose on them to pay for the French and Indian War.

McIntosh had sent the eighth Pennsylvania regiment, under Colonel Daniel Brodhead and the thirteenth Virginia regiment under Colonel John Gibson, along with two regiments of Virginia militia to start building the first fort on Delaware land. Lt

Colonel White Eyes - he was given an army rank to lead the expedition - and the experienced guide Bobby Bee led the soldiers along the Ohio River towards Beaver River, followed by the usual camp followers of merchants, laundresses, and ladies of the night. McIntosh stayed behind to finish his work on planning and obtaining the necessary funds and supplies for the operation. He would catch up to them later.

At the new fort site, Gibson and Brodhead found that to get anything done at all, they had to have the Pennsylvania Continentals work on one project, the Virginia Continentals on another, and left it up to the militia captains to assign the work for their men. Otherwise, fighting broke out, and nothing got done. So the Pennsylvania soldiers cut the trees and rolled them to the building site, the militiamen dug the trench, and the Virginia soldiers planted the logs to make a palisade.

"How come we have to do the hard work?" Lewis complained to nobody in particular.

"You'd rather fell trees?" asked the man digging next to him.

"Well, no."

"Then shut up, kid, and dig. This is easy stuff. Don't be a shagbag."

While the fort was being built, everyone slept in tents. Many mornings, the air was thick with fog and dew, so the men were allowed to remain in their tents with their guns at the ready until muster. Evenings, once work was done, fights broke out.

The militia, three-month men, weren't used to the military discipline of being told when to get up, go to bed, and stand watches. They often ignored orders. Militia officers wouldn't obey the Continental officers and vice versa. Colonel Gibson and Colonel Brodhead held almost daily courts-martial. Usually, the punishment was a whipping.

Alcohol added to the problems. The merchants that followed the army had a captive clientele, and the price of whiskey doubled and then tripled once they were on the trail. They claimed they had higher expenses, which was true. They had to hire wagons and pay drivers. Some of the soldiers had money, some didn't. The Continentals hadn't been paid in months, and they were jealous as they watched the whiskey merchants and women hang around the militia camps, where some of the militiamen paid for whiskey and services in Spanish silver dollars.

Although the soldiers didn't get along, they all feared Indian attack. The fort went up quickly as all the men, Continentals and militiamen, with the help of the camp followers, raced each other to get the fort built and get out of their tents and behind the safety of palisades and thick log walls.

Brodhead and Gibson, experienced officers from the French and Indian War, knew enough about Chief White Eyes that they weren't worried about an Indian attack. They liked and trusted White Eyes and figured they were safe in Delaware territory. Gibson, although busy with the problems of his men, often stopped by White Eyes camp in the evenings to exchange pleasantries. He had been a fur trader until he was captured during Pontiac's Rebellion and had been adopted into the Lenape tribe. He had learned their ways and their language. Visiting Chief White Eyes was his brief refuge in the evening away from the problems of his command.

White Eyes, who kept his camp away from the loud and unruly whites, was always happy to have the company and kept some morsels of food on hand, whether rabbit, quail, turkey, or venison to offer Gibson, unaware that he was expected to feed all the troops.

Meanwhile, General McIntosh was having his own difficulties back at Fort Pitt. He was a rigid, by-the-book leader, and he immediately butted heads with not only his Continentals but even more so with the militia, who saw themselves as a free and democratic people fighting for their freedom not only from a king and a pope, but also anybody else who tried to lord it over them, including him. McIntosh found many of the officers insubordinate.

At daily muster, McIntosh was surprised so many of his Continentals who were supposed to be on duty were absent without leave. And the militiamen were even worse. He demanded to know why.

The excuses he got were wide and varied. He was told things like "Private Kelly was homesick and wanted to see his Ma and Pa," or Private Hoaglin went to help his family bring in the corn harvest," or "Sargent Smith said he isn't mustering until he gets his back pay," or "the whole squad went hunting because they were hungry, sir," or even "Private DeWitt fell in love with a harlot, sir," or "the men were up late partying, sir, so I let them sleep in."

McIntosh was livid. He ordered that no one was to leave the post for any reason.

"But, sir," asked one militia commander. "What about liberty? The men stand their watches, they do what we ask of them. They expect to be able to go into town and blow off a little steam."

"Liberty is cancelled," McIntosh fumed. The soldiers who had to enforce that order were as unhappy as the soldiers who tried to leave the post.

The news of an American army heading into the Ohio country towards the Beaver River spread quickly. Knotche, Black Snake, and Goose heard the news while they were at Pluggy's Town, where they had gone after the attempt to scalp Lewis Wetzel had gone awry. The Half King Dunquat was sending out war belts, asking the tribes to attack the American army, who were getting too close to the Wyandot villages. Although the Lenape built homes and farmed around Coshocton, it was at the invitation of the Wyandot, who claimed the land as their own. To Knotche, the army coming closer was the perfect opportunity to avenge the death of his mother. The three friends agreed to go to the Beaver River to do their part.

"That was a long walk for nothing," Goose complained. *"We should have just stayed home. It would have been a lot closer. Instead, we walked all over and we've got nothing to show for it."* Goose wasn't happy to go home empty-handed. If he was ever going to persuade Danelle to be his wife, he had

to come up with a suitable dowry. The second raid on the Wetzel cabin had produced very little of value.

"Things haven't been going well," Knotche agreed. *"We lost two good warriors. We've got no horses, although we almost had them. We tried to catch the boy whose gun is always loaded but failed. I wish I had stayed in Kuskuskee. I'd be better off. Kuskuskee isn't far from where the Long Knife army is."*

"I'm up for some adventure," Black Snake said. *"I say we go pay the Long Knife army a visit."*

They headed down the Cuyahoga Trail towards the Lenape towns, where they hoped to find shelter and food. Before they knew it, the dogs at Coshocton started barking, and armed warriors surrounded them. They were prevented from going any farther by the war chief Hopocan.

"We have made a treaty with the Americans," Hopocan told Knotche and his men. *"We have given them free passage across our land. No war parties. I would join you myself if that were not the case."*

Knotche begged Hopocan. *"I am just asking for my rights to take revenge on the Long Knives who killed my mother at Kuskuskee."*

Hopocan was startled when he heard that news. *"Your mother was killed? At Kuskuskee? My brother was also killed there by those devils. And they wounded my elderly mother. I am so sorry for your loss, my brother."*

Knotche, too, was surprised when he heard Hopocan's report. *"And I am sorry for your loss as well, my brother."* Knotche had known Hopocan was a Munsee, but their paths had rarely crossed.

With that turn of events, being denied access to cross Lenape land, Knotche's plan of harassing the

Long Knives' army fell apart. Hopocan invited them to stay with him in his village. Hopocan treated them as honored guests and saw that they were comfortable and well looked after for several days. While there, enjoying his hospitality, Hopocan told them, *"I do not trust these white men coming near our villages."*

"Those Long Knives can't be trusted," agreed Knotche. *"I would bet on it."*

"That is a wager I will not take," Black Snake added, *"no matter what the odds are."*

They both looked at Goose. *"No, no. I'm not betting on that. But I am up for a game of chuck-a-luck."* He rattled the dice.

Hopocan put his hand on Knotche's shoulder. *"Perhaps you will honor me by helping me keep an eye on those white devils. But no scalps. If you find a horse or two, though, or other "lost" goods, you are welcome to claim them,"* said Hopocan.

"You are a true friend," Knotche replied, with a big grin. *"It would be our honor to do this task."* Black Snake and Goose also readily agreed.

Hopocan told them where the Long Knife army could be found and described a good spot to spy on them without being seen.

They agreed to go after a few days' rest. Knotche planned to keep on the trail east. Hopocan, though, told them it was far shorter to take a different trail, and he even agreed to walk with them to the turnoff, which he did. He drew them a map in the dirt. The weather was pleasant as the three old friends headed down the trail marked out by Hopocan. They stopped often to roll the dice or take naps.

The army was easy to find. They heard the noise from a couple of miles off as trees fell, shaking the ground, and as they got closer, they heard yelling. They didn't get too close, and they were very careful. There were too many eyes, and the white warriors were too unpredictable. They were running all over the place. Twice, they had a chance to take the scalps from deserters, but they had promised Hopocan that they would not, so they let them pass unmolested.

Knotche and his men watched as Fort McIntosh was built. They watched the conflicts. It was very entertaining to watch the fights, making bets upon the outcomes. The whippings, though, shocked all three of them. They had never seen anything like that. They had seen cruelty to one's enemies, but this was something different altogether. The men whipped usually cried and begged for the punishment to stop.

"These whites really are evil," Goose remarked. *"Imagine whipping a man like that. They are cruel."*

"Yes," Black Snake agreed. *"It gives me pain just to watch it. But the whites are cowards. I would never cry and beg for it to stop. I would tell them, 'Go ahead. Do it harder.'"*

"They have not learned to be human," said Knotche. *"They look human, but they don't act like it."*

They had been watching the Long Knives build the fort for a week when Black Snake spotted Lewis Wetzel. *"That's the boy whose rifle is always loaded,"* he whispered, pointing at Lewis digging with a shovel.

"No, that can't be," Knotche said. He followed Black Snake's outstretched finger.

Goose came running over to see, too. Lewis was wearing trousers, but with no shirt. His long black hair was tied in a bun at the nape of his neck. His face and chest were sweaty and streaked with dirt. There were several other militiamen in a line digging holes. *"What's he doing here?"*

"Who cares," Black Snake replied. *"It's a clear shot. I can get him."* He started notching an arrow. Goose ran to get his musket.

"No!" Said Knotche. *"I want his scalp, too. But I gave my word to Hopocan. We all did."*

8 MURDER

General McIntosh finally set out from Fort Pitt in late October to catch up with Colonels Brodhead and Gibson. He marched with twelve-hundred men, half of them militiamen. Sixty of them were employed as officers' servants. Not all the supplies he needed had arrived yet. He was still expecting a herd of beef cattle. He left Colonel Richard Campbell in charge of Fort Pitt, with one-hundred-fifty men, and ordered that Campbell forward the cattle as soon as they arrived.

The construction of Fort McIntosh was proceeding at a fast pace by the time McIntosh and his troops arrived at the site. He immediately instituted orders to tighten up military discipline. Revelry was held at first light, rather than eight o'clock. The troops had thirty minutes to eat, then they were to muster at their work sites. Since food supplies were still low, he ordered rations cut back further. The soldiers objected. McIntosh convened daily courts-martial for any law and order violations, and even the civilians were included in those proceedings.

A soldier from the eighth Pennsylvania regiment received two-hundred lashes for stealing money from a militiaman. It was cut to one hundred when he returned the money.

A militiaman was charged with being drunk on duty. Two hundred lashes.

Captain McConnick of the thirteenth Virginia Regiment was charged with disobeying an order and being absent without leave. He was ordered discharged from the service, but McIntosh ordered him returned to duty with a warning.

Two pack horse drivers were charged with theft, but no evidence was produced, and they were released.

Knotche and his men watched but had no way of knowing what was really going on. Knotche understood some English, but they couldn't hear most of the proceedings. What they saw was appalling to them.

Chief White Eyes went to General McIntosh's tent the evening of his arrival. The Chief shook the general's hand. He told McIntosh, with Gibson translating, that this was the land of the Lenape and the soldiers were disrespecting it. He could understand why they needed to cut down trees in order to build a great fort, but the trees were crying out to him. The soldiers were carving their initials into the trees, and it had to stop.

McIntosh demanded to know where the food was that the Delaware had promised. He ordered Lt Colonel White Eyes to get his Indians to start bringing in meat for his soldiers. White Eyes didn't know what he was talking about, but assured him that his people would be happy to trade. Of course, McIntosh didn't have anything to trade with and couldn't understand why this Indian wouldn't live up to his side of the bargain he'd made at the Treaty.

Colonel Gibson explained that there must be some sort of misunderstanding. Chief White Eyes didn't know he'd agreed to feed McIntosh's soldiers. They had their own families to feed. McIntosh was surprised by that information.

65

McIntosh thought that White Eyes was crazy for complaining about men carving their initials on trees. There were trees all over. But he also wanted to appease him since his army was on Delaware land, and he needed Delaware help. McIntosh announced at muster the next day that anyone damaging a tree that wasn't being used to build the fort would receive twenty-five lashes. There was no doubt in anyone's mind where and how that order had originated.

A few days later, towards evening, Chief White Eyes was reported seen by several soldiers carrying a handful of quail over to his camp. Colonel Gibson went by for his nightly visit, carrying a lantern through the woods to White Eyes' camp. One of his servants had cooked some sweet cornpones, and he thought White Eyes would enjoy one. It wasn't night yet, but the sun was low, and it was dark in the big forest with a canopy that totally blocked out the light. Bloodthirsty mosquitoes circled around and dove at the lantern light. Gibson smelled cooking meat as he neared the camp and thought it an odd smell. As he walked into the small clearing of the Chief's camp, he saw White Eyes sprawled across his own campfire. The flesh of his arm was black and sizzling in the coals. Most of the fire was smothered by the body. There was a bloody, pinkish patch on the top of his head, though most of his long, grey hair was still intact but caked with blood.

Gibson ran over and pulled him from the fire. White Eyes' eyeglasses fell off into the fire-pit. He turned White Eyes over onto his back. His grey eyes were partially hidden by his half-closed eyelids. His prominent nose drooped to one side, and the sides of his mouth were pulled back into a grimace revealing perfectly white teeth. His skin was cool and clammy.

Gibson was shocked. He looked all around the campsite, but there was no sign of anybody. White Eyes' little bark wigwam looked intact. Gibson was cool-headed. If word got out that Chief White Eyes had been murdered, there would be hell to pay. They needed that fort. And they needed it supplied. They would need it even more if word got out about the murder of the Lenape chief. They were on Lenape land, and they were no match for thousands of angry Lenape warriors who knew the lay of this land. He hurried straight to General McIntosh's tent. McIntosh was talking to Colonel Brodhead about the shortage of food. Gibson spouted out the news.

"God-damn it! That's all we need!" McIntosh yelled, slamming his fist on his cot. "Muster the men right now. We'll get to the bottom of this. Whoever did this is going to hang! God-damn it!" Spittle went flying.

"But, sir," Gibson said. "We can't do that. If the Delaware find out one of our men murdered their chief, there'll be hell to pay."

McIntosh grabbed his head and rolled his eyes. "Jesus Christ! This is madness!"

The two colonels, both experienced in the native ways, convinced their General that they needed to get the word out without unleashing a hornet's nest of angry Indians. McIntosh listened to his two colonels. Gibson knew Indians. He had lived with them. Brodhead was a tough, seasoned fighter. Together, they made a plan. They decided that the best thing to do would be to bury the body quickly before anybody had a chance to examine it, and send an express messenger to the Delaware with word that Chief White Eyes had died of natural causes.

"Tell them it was small-pox," suggested Gibson. "That way, they won't want to even see the body."

"Who else knows?" Brodhead asked.

"Just us and the killer," Gibson replied.

"Somebody probably saw or heard something," said the General. "It's that God-damn militia. I know it!"

"Well, we can't ask around," said Brodhead. "Otherwise, everyone will soon know he's dead. I doubt the killer or killers will be talking, but if they do, they'll be making a big mistake. We'll hang the bloody murderers!"

Knotche and his men suspected something was going on by the sudden change of activity but had no idea what.

Captain McConnick was selected personally by General McIntosh to deliver the message to the Delaware. It was a chance for McConnick to redeem himself after his court-martial. It was a dangerous mission and could easily turn deadly. McConnick and his company of Continentals rode down the wide streets into the peaceful Moravian settlement of Gnadenhutten, which was Gibson's idea. They were warmly greeted by the missionaries.

One of the missionaries, John Heckewelder, accompanied them to Coshocton with a white flag. Soldiers with guns had never been seen in the Lenape capital, and armed warriors quickly surrounded them. Heckewelder called for a council meeting. Heckewelder was a man of substance to the Lenape and was highly respected. Word was sent out to the surrounding villages.

The next day, the chiefs and important warriors filed into the long house, White Eyes' home, and took their places along the walls. Chief Killbuck took the place at the head where Chief White Eyes would have sat. Next to him sat the war chief Hopocan.

When they were all seated and the pipe passed around for everyone to share in the same smoke, Captain McConnick addressed the leaders of the tribe. Heckewelder translated.

"Brothers," McConnick said. "I have brought sad news from General McIntosh. Your great chief, and the good friend of the Americans, Chief White Eyes, has passed away to the great hunting ground in the sky."

There were moans and cries and shrieks. Eyes peeking through the cracks from outside disappeared and, there were cries and the sounds of running feet as the word spread throughout the village.

When the room quieted down, Killbuck asked, "Tell us, my friend, how did it come about that our great chief has died?"

McConnick, who knew only what he had been told, what he thought was the truth, said, "Chief White Eyes died from smallpox. We had to bury him so that the disease wouldn't spread."

Hopocan, with great concern in his voice, said in English, "That is a terrible disease. How many died?"

"Sir?" asked McConnick.

"How many more people died of this terrible affliction? How many of your warriors caught this terrible disease? It is very contagious."

"No one else, sir," said McConnick.

Hopocan's eyes grew wide in disbelief. "None? No others died?"

"No, sir. Just Chief White Eyes."

"I have been around smallpox many times," said Hopocan softly, in his own language, as if he remembered the devastation smallpox had caused to his people all his life. *"I have never heard of something like this. Only one man, our great chief White Eyes, a friend to the Americans, died of this terrible disease.*

9 FORT LAURENS

McIntosh wasted no time. The murder of Chief White Eyes heightened his resolve. He needed to get these forts built and destroy the British fort at Detroit before his whole enterprise unraveled. He marched his twelve-hundred troops on a trek north starting on November fourth, with Bobby Bee leading the way. They needed to find another building site quickly, another fort a few days march closer to the British. But they no longer had an expert like White Eyes to show them the best spot.

As soon as they saw General McIntosh proceeding northward, Knotche knew they had to make a report to Hopocan. They had no idea that Chief White Eyes had been killed.

Before they left, to make their return trip easier, they made a night-time visit to the corral where the camp-followers kept their horses. This was the sort of fun Black Snake loved, and he volunteered to go in first.

He blackened his face from the charcoals of their fire. He waited until the early morning, before first light. He picked a handful of sweetgrass in each hand. While he slithered into the corral, Knotche and Goose opened the gate slightly without making a sound and waited with halters they had woven earlier in the day out of wild hemp.

Black Snake brought over one horse at a time, and his two friends, upon receiving a horse, led them away from the camp. Black Snake came out last with the horse he wanted. By dawn, they were twenty miles away.

They reported to Hopocan that a large army, with their big chief, was heading north. Hopocan rode out to see the Long Knife Army himself, since the direction they were heading was not far from Coshocton. Knotche, Black Snake, and Goose joined him on their new horses, along with a band of Lenape warriors.

The army headed northward, following the Indian trail towards the lake and Indian towns there. The weather was getting colder, and winter would soon be upon them. When General McIntosh reached the Tuscarawa valley, he recognized the area from what he'd read about in the British Colonel Bouquet's treaty twenty years before. Bouquet had held a treaty with the Seneca, Shawnee, and Delaware there and demanded that they return their white captives after Pontiac's Rebellion. He saw the benefits of building a fort on that site, things that Bouquet had undoubtedly seen, too. The spot would control traffic on the Tuscarawa River. Maybe supplies could be sent down the river to the Ohio River and then back up to Fort Pitt. It wasn't too far from the Delaware villages, and it wasn't far from the lake Indian towns, either, nor far from Fort Detroit. McIntosh ordered his soldiers to begin building another protective fort right away.

The new fort on the Tuscarawa River was named Fort Laurens in honor of the president of the Continental Congress, who had been McIntosh's mentor when he was a young man in the south. Henry Laurens had given McIntosh a job in his counting-house and had helped him on the road to financial success. Work on the fort began immediately.

Back at Fort McIntosh, the cattle McIntosh had requisitioned as a food supply for his troops had finally arrived from Fort Pitt. The cooks butchered some, but there were far more than they needed. They had no salt to cure it, so they kept the cattle alive. They would send them on to General McIntosh when he asked for them, as he ordered. A messenger was sent telling him of their arrival. Meanwhile, since they had no feed for them at Fort McIntosh, the cattle were driven to Raccoon Creek to fend for themselves on the thick brush and willow, just before the first frost killed the forage.

10 WOLF HUNTING

Once the building of Fort McIntosh was completed and the General, with most of the Continental soldiers, had gone north, the militiamen were left to guard the fort. There wasn't much to do. There was no sign of any Indians. They had guard duty, sometimes latrine duty or kitchen duty or firewood duty, but mostly, they had plenty of free time.

Lewis and Billy stood their watches and did their assigned duties. Lewis swore he'd never join the army again and was all for running off, but the whippings that deserters received when they were caught made him think otherwise. And they knew who he was, so there was no escaping. But the worst would be trying to explain deserting to his father.

They were allowed to hunt and fish when they weren't on duty, and both boys were happy to do that all day long, every day, though the hunting was poor. Too many hunters and not enough game.

"What day is it?" Lewis asked Billy. "We only signed up till Christmas."

"We've got seven more days and a wake-up."

"I wish I were home," said Lewis. "I can't stand being cooped up like this. Wanna go run around tonight and have a little fun?"

"You're crazy. If injuns don't get us, then the sergeant will. He'll think we're deserting and want to paint some stripes on our backs. No, thanks."

They heard wolves howling.

"Good for nothing wolves," said Billy. "I hate them critters more than anything."

"I had a couple following me the other night," said Lewis. "I thought they was injuns. Gave me the creeps. I'd stop and hide and wait for them to catch up, figuring I'd get me a scalp. They'd stop, too. I'd have never known it was wolves if I hadn't surprised a deer. It took off, and them dang wolves ran right on past me after it!"

"They catch it?"

"Yeah, probably. I didn't stick around."

"My pa said he saw one caught in a deer trap one time. An injun trap. They dug a hole on a deer trail and laid branches over it. Idea was that a deer comes walking along and 'bam!' It steps on the twigs and leaves covering up the hole, and it falls right in."

"Must be a deep hole," said Lewis. "And narrow, too, else it would just jump out."

"I reckon. A wolf was down in it, trying to get out."

"With a deer?"

"Naw. It just fell in. He came on it, and it was trying to scramble up the sides. My pa smashed its head with a rock."

"There's a lot of dang wolves around here."

"I'll bet they're eating those cattle down on Coon Creek."

"What a stupid waste of good meat."

"What'd' ya expect from the army?"

Lewis looked at Billy. "I'd like to try catching a wolf. Wanna see if we can catch one? I'd love to teach one of them buggers a lesson."

"With an injun deer trap? Sure!"

The two teenagers went to the commissary and asked the cook for some cattle guts for bait. They had been regularly stopping in to get fishing bait and shared their catch with him, so the cook was glad to share his garbage.

From the gear locker, they requisitioned two shovels and a couple of buckets.

They picked a spot to dig the trap in a meadow down near Raccoon Creek, thinking that there would be fewer roots there and plenty of wolves.

It took them all day to dig a hole deep enough. They both dug at first, but once it got deep enough, they took turns digging. While one of them shoveled dirt into a bucket, the other would hoist the bucket and empty it. They dug it so that it was higher than the top of Lewis' head, over six feet. The sides were as straight as they could make them, but it wasn't even long enough to lay down in, and barely three feet wide.

Billy pulled Lewis out, and they dropped cattle waste – ears, lungs, and boney parts with a little meat still left on it – to the bottom. They covered the hole with light twigs and a layer of leaves, guessing that was probably the way the Indians did it to catch deer. It was nearly dark when they walked back to the fort. They both had night watches.

The next day, they went back to check on their trap.

As they neared the hole, they could hear something moving around in it. "I knew it! I knew we could catch a dang wolf!" said Billy.

Lewis crept up to the edge and looked down. A young, grey female wolf was pawing at the sides, trying to get out of the hole. She growled and showed her teeth when Lewis's face appeared.

"Now, what do we do? Target practice?" Billy asked, looking over Lewis' shoulder.

"That ain't sportin'," said Lewis. "We ain't murderers. Got to at least give her a sportin' chance."

"Yeah, like how?" asked Billy.

"Jump down there with that wolf, one on one. Just you and your knife."

"You're crazy!" said Billy. "I ain't jumping into a hole with a dang wolf."

"If you're chicken, then I'll do it."

"I ain't chicken. That's just crazy, is all."

"You got an old deerskin or blanket you don't mind giving up?" Lewis asked.

"I suppose."

"Go get it. And bring some rawhide, too. I'll wait here and keep an eye on this critter to make sure she don't get away."

Billy took off running. When he got back with his bundle, he handed it to Lewis.

"What are you aiming to do?"

"Watch. Load your rifle, just in case."

Lewis watched while Billy loaded his rifle.

Stuffing the rawhide strips into his belt, Lewis picked up the deerskin and draped it down in front of him, holding it out like a shield. He lightly leaped into the hole, right on top of the wolf's back. The wolf collapsed to the ground under his weight, then struggled to turn her head, growling and snapping, but Lewis wrapped the deerskin quickly around her head and held onto it with both arms. There was muffled growling and paws scrambling and pushing, trying to get loose. The young wolf struggled to get away, but Lewis held tight. Lewis was light and wiry, but he still outweighed her by three to one. He inched himself up until he was lying on her head. She struggled to get up with her hind legs but couldn't. With one hand, he wrapped a strip of rawhide around one hind leg, then pulled it towards the other and wrapped both legs tightly. She struggled to get free. He held on tight, pinning her head to the ground with his bodyweight. He did the same with the front legs. Afterwards, he tied the deerskin around her neck so that she couldn't see or bite.

"If that ain't the darnest thing I ever saw!" said Billy. "You've hogtied a dang wolf!"

"You ain't seen nothing yet," said Lewis. He was breathing heavy, and he was covered with sweat. "I'm going to teach this wolf, and every other wolf, not to mess with Lewis Wetzel."

He stood up. The wolf struggled to get to her feet but couldn't. Lewis put his foot on her to hold her down. He pulled out his knife.

With Billy watching, wide-eyed and grimacing, Lewis proceeded to skin the wolf alive, starting at her hind legs. She growled and barked and struggled at first.

"Get down here and hold her still," Lewis ordered.

There was barely enough room. Billy lowered himself down. There was only enough room for the wolf and the two of them standing or sitting on top of it. Billy kneeled onto the wolf's neck. Lewis sat on her rear. The wolf whimpered while Lewis used the point of his knife to loosen the fur and skin and then yanked, pulling back large swaths of fur and skin.

The poor wolf struggled at first, snarling and trying to lunge at Billy through the deerskin, but it was caught firmly in the two boys' vice-like grip. She whimpered, then gave up and lay quietly while Lewis worked his knife, loosening up the skin and yanking it back. There was very little bleeding. Billy pulled the deerskin out of the way as Lewis skinned. Working together, they skinned the wolf on both sides. They left the belly and the head and neck untouched.

"That ought to do her," said Lewis. He wiped the blade clean on the pile of fur and slipped the knife back into its sheath at his side. "You lift that end, I'll get this one."

Billy slipped one arm under the wolf's neck. "I'm ready."

"One . . . two . . . three!" Together, they raised it over their heads and tossed it out of the hole. It landed with a thud.

"Here!" Lewis held out his cupped hands, and Billy stood in them, and Lewis boosted him out of the hole. Then, Billy reached down with his hand and pulled Lewis up.

They thought the wolf would take off running once they untied the deerskin from its head, but it didn't. It wasn't dead but just lay there whimpering.

"We should put that poor critter out of its misery," said Billy.

"And what will the other wolves learn from that?" Lewis said. "This here sends a message to them to stay out of our way."

They sat there for a while watching the wolf but soon got bored.

"I'm hungry," said Billy.

"Me, too.

The two teenagers left the wolf lying there to die.

11 TROUBLE

While construction of Fort Laurens was underway, General McIntosh sent word to the Delaware at Coshocton and the Mingo and Wyandot chiefs at the lake towns. He told them to come to the new fort to discuss a treaty. He would start talks in fourteen days, trying to time it so that there was no time wasted. Food was in short supply, so there were considerable urgency and speed required. He hoped to have the fort built by then. He sent a messenger to Fort McIntosh to send up food supplies. He barely had enough time, if everything went smoothly, for the Indians to get to the site, food to arrive from Fort McIntosh to feed them, and hold a treaty talks in time to get the militia home by Christmas, when their enlistments ran out. There was no time to spare.

His message to the Indians was blunt. "If any nations or tribes refuse this offer now, I will never make it again, nor rest, nor leave this country, but pursue them while any of them remain upon the face of the earth, for I can fill the woods with as many men as there are trees in the forest or stones on the ground."

Half King Dunquat laughed at the ultimatum.

Hopocan thought it an odd demand from a friend. Neither Fort McIntosh nor Fort Laurens were what he had asked for at the Fort Pitt Treaty when he had given his approval to the Americans to build these forts. His people needed to trade, and they needed protection from the British and their native allies. Neither of these forts offered either one. Fort McIntosh offered nothing. It was too far away from their villages. Fort Laurens was close enough to Coshocton for the Lenape to trade their furs for necessary supplies but too far away to offer any protection for his people from the British and their allies, the Wyandot and the Iroquois. Hopocan was beginning to doubt whether the Americans could even supply the needs of his people. They had yet to trade anything. When Knotche reported that the American troops didn't seem to be well provisioned and that many of the soldiers were dressed in rags, he had to see it for himself.

Hopocan and his band of Lenape warriors, with Knotche, Black Snake, and Goose pointing things out, watched from the woods outside the new Fort Laurens as it was being built. They came daily to observe what was going on with the American army as fall turned into winter and the snow fell. They could see that McIntosh's army wasn't equipped for cold weather. Their clothes were threadbare, and the soldiers were sending out hunting parties daily and not finding much. Like White Eyes, he was unaware that he'd agreed to supply food to the army, and he didn't have the excuse that he didn't understand English. But he couldn't read or write it, and he had put his X on the Fort Pitt Treaty agreeing to it. But Hopocan balked at befriending the Long Knives, of feeding them, though he could see for himself they needed help. He didn't trust them. He wondered how they could possibly help his people when they couldn't even help themselves.

No food arrived from Fort McIntosh, so McIntosh sent a company back down to bring up the cattle. But once the snow had fallen, the cattle at Raccoon Creek had starved to death, and the wolves, vultures, and eagles had left very little. Rather than return empty-handed, McIntosh's company loaded up the hides since they needed leather at Fort Laurens as well.

When the day of this new treaty arrived, the General had no presents to offer to the few chiefs and warriors who showed up, which the British and Spanish always freely gave. There was no banquet, either. No food had arrived.

Hopocan wasn't the only Lenape leader starting to wonder if aligning with the Americans was such a good idea. White Eyes had always defended the Americans, believing that aligning with them was in the Lenapes' best interests. That's why he wanted a fourteenth state for his people. But with him dead, the Americans no longer had their major supporter among the Lenape. With winter coming on, the Lenape had been expecting gifts of blankets and clothes, which they sorely needed. They were even willing to pay for those items with furs, but the Americans had none to trade. The native delegations drifted back to their homes without agreeing to anything.

British envoys and Half King Dunquat visited Coshocton and urged the Lenape, once again, to join with him against the Americans.

At Fort Laurens, rations were cut from one and a half pounds of flour per day for each man to one-quarter pound. Knotche, Black Snake, and Goose were having a hard time, too. It was unfamiliar territory to them, and they weren't the only ones trying to feed themselves from the sparse game near the fort. Not only were the Lenape towns and their hunters nearby, but the soldiers, too, sent out hunting parties.

"I wish I were home ice fishing," grumbled Goose. *"We could be fat and happy."*

Knotche was wishing he had someplace to go. He no longer had a family to go home to. He had agreed to Hopocan's request to watch the fort, so that was his fate, but he wished there was something more. Even with his two friends, he was lonely and sad. Winter wasn't a time to be hanging around a white man's fort. The palisades were up, and the walls were on the fort, and he could hear the chopping and yelling and cursing, and it made him depressed.

"I'm going to find us something to eat," Black Snake announced. *"I'm not going to just sit here while those soldiers are snug and warm in their fancy fort."* He grabbed his bow and arrows and trotted off to the south.

"I'll go with you," Knotche said. *"Just to make sure we get something."* Patting his amulet, he ran to catch up.

McIntosh gave orders for the main army to prepare to march home, leaving one-hundred-fifty men under Colonel Gibson to finish building the fort. Christmas was fast approaching - it was four days off, and they were one-hundred-thirty miles from Fort Pitt. Militia enlistments were expiring on December 25. For their last supper before departing, McIntosh's soldiers boiled the cattle hides that had been sent to them to make leather repairs. The General left Gibson and his men with two days of provisions. They marched out in the morning with the thirteenth Virginia regiment and part of the eighth Pennsylvania regiment. Leading each company was a fifer and a drummer. Rather than the orderly march back McIntosh had ordered and expected, soon the hungry soldiers refused to obey orders from anybody. They took off running, some following the trail, some cutting overland.

It was more orderly at Fort McIntosh. Two days before their enlistments were due to expire, Lewis and Billy, along with the rest of the militiamen, marched back to Fort Pitt.

12 STARVATION

Most of the Continental soldiers and many of the eligible young men in the Western district had gone on McIntosh's fort building expedition. Taking advantage of the lack of fighting men in the vicinity, Seneca warriors from the upper Allegheny raided the outlying settlements around Fort Pitt. Pennsylvania hadn't mustered its militia for McIntosh's expedition. All volunteers had joined the Virginia militia. Pennsylvania called for its own militia to muster, to attack and destroy the Seneca villages. The Pennsylvania militia mustered and marched up alongside the Allegheny River, intent on revenge, before running into severe winter weather. They were still ten miles from the first Seneca village when the hungry, miserable militiamen voted that this was a bad idea, and they scurried back home.

It was worse for the soldiers at Fort Laurens. They were starving. Private Nash, who had been with Captain McConnick's company when he delivered the message about Chief White Eyes' death to the Lenape, volunteered to go to the Lenape villages to buy food.

"Give this note to one of the missionaries," Colonel Gibson told him. He handed Nash a letter that explained the army's desperate situation. He wrote that he had no funds, but the debt, he assured the missionary, would be paid by the full faith and credit of the United States of America, the name the rebelling colonies had been calling themselves since September of 1776. Gibson called upon the missionary to ask the converts to help out their Christian brothers. He was certain, he assured him, that his IOU would be honored by General McIntosh.

The Lenape had been wavering in their support for the Americans and were now leaning towards the British. Now, with White Eyes dead, the war chief Hopocan was denouncing them.

They are weak," Hopocan pointed out at council. "I've been watching them. They have nothing. No food. No clothing." He held up the Half King's black wampum belt, urging the Lenape to join the Wyandot in supporting the British. "We need to align with the strong, not the weak if we are to survive."

Private Nash made the mistake of walking directly into the traditional Lenape village of Coshocton, rather than the Christian town of Gnadenhutten nearby. He never made it to the council house. Barking dogs alerted everyone of his arrival. When Lenape warriors spotted this armed soldier, he was shot and scalped before he got within a hundred yards.

Knotche, Black Snake, and Goose were watching Fort Laurens. Black Snake was getting to be a pretty good shot with rabbits if they stayed still but rarely hit anything else. Goose was setting traps for raccoons, but there weren't many. Nearly every morning, the traps were empty. Knotche had managed to shoot a deer, so they weren't starving. Mostly, they were bored and spent much of the day playing chuck-a-luck next to their fire if they had something to eat.

The renegade Simon Girty, leading a war party of Seneca and Cayuga of the Iroquois Nation, showed up at Coshocton. He had been sent from Fort Detroit to observe the American activity. Girty had been General Hand's guide the previous year during the Squaw Campaign and, after deserting, had allied with the British. Hopocan guided Girty's party to Knotche's camp. Girty made camp with them.

Soon after Girty's arrival, sharp-eyed Black Snake spotted American hunters returning with a heavy load of meat. Miraculously, one of Colonel Gibson's provisioning parties had found both a wood buffalo and an elk. They shot and skinned both of them, cut them into pieces, and loaded on their backs all they could carry. Hopocan signaled for Knotche and his men to circle around ahead of the hunters and hide behind trees while he and Girty's warriors attacked from the rear. Peace with the weak Americans was over.

Hopocan whooped loudly and ordered the attack. The soldiers took off, running as fast as they could right towards Knotche's waiting men. Black Snake wounded one with a lucky arrow shot to a soldier's butt. The man fell head over heels spilling meat all over the snow. Black Snake grabbed him by the neck and threatened him with his tomahawk. The man held up his hands in surrender. Black Snake took him prisoner. One of Girty's warriors caught another from behind with his tomahawk and scalped him. Knotche stepped from behind a big maple right into the path of Private Frank Enfield, who was running as fast as he could with one-hundred pounds of buffalo meat on his back.

"This is for my mother!" Knotche yelled as he swung his tomahawk sideways into Enfield's neck, nearly severing his head.

The other soldiers ran right past Goose after his shot nicked a branch, sending it falling to the ground. They escaped after dropping their loads and racing back through the gates. All their meat windfall was left behind in the snow.

"I'm glad to have this," Goose said, picking through one bundle. *"I'm starting to lose weight."* He was more than starting. He had no belly anymore.

Everyone else was glad to get it, too. Girty's force of Indians had been traveling light, and suddenly, there was enough food for everybody.

The Continental soldier captured by Black Snake recognized Girty.

"It's bad," the private told Girty. "We've got nothing to eat. We're starving. The men are sick of it. They want to leave. It's the holiday season, you know? Some Christmas!"

Girty sent a messenger to the British at Fort Detroit with word of the Americans' plight.

Two weeks after General McIntosh departed, the soldiers at Fort Laurens mutinied. They had nothing to eat. It was the middle of winter, and they were freezing cold, and they couldn't safely leave the fort even for firewood. They also hadn't been paid since the start of this expedition – not that there was any place to spend their money. They refused to follow the orders of their officers.

"We're leaving," one of the privates in the mob at the gate told Colonel Gibson, "and you can't stop us. You know what you can do with your army, sir!" He pointed at his rear end.

"What about them?" Gibson looked down upon them from one of the watchtowers. He was holding a loaded musket in one hand. He pointed to the smoke of fires in the woods outside the fort.

"We ain't afraid of them. Let them try to stop us. We'll kill the buggers. We're going to starve to death here. At least we've got a fighting chance out there."

Another private said, "Enough talk. Come on, let's get out of here." He started to lift the log that held the gate closed.

Colonel Gibson looked down on them. "I've got three loaded muskets up here," he said. "Open that gate, and the first three men out are dead men. And I can reload pretty damn quick, too. Go right ahead, private."

"You wouldn't dare," he replied. "You'd shoot one of your own?"

Gibson stared at the private. He wasn't smiling. "Try me, bud." He pulled back the hammer with his thumb. It clicked. "Now back away from that gate if you know what's good for you."

The private set the log back down and backed up. "You're crazy," he said to Gibson. He looked around at the others. Nearly the entire garrison had their blankets on their backs and their muskets on their shoulders, ready to flee.

"I ain't going first," the private said and melted back into the crowd.

"We could shoot you, Colonel. We've all got muskets, too," said one man.

"You can try," Gibson said coolly. "Likely, you'll succeed, too. Eventually. You willing to load your musket? Go ahead. Load your musket, mister."

No one moved. Minutes went by. Everyone's eyes shifted around at each other. No one dared move a muscle.

Suddenly, there was a sharp pounding on the outside of the gate. "Open up! Hurry up! We got a deer! It's me, Private John Frazier!"

Gibson glanced quickly over the palisade, still holding his musket pointing into the crowd. "All of you. Back away from the gate. You there." Gibson pointed his musket at a sergeant. "Open the gate."

The men did as they were told and backed away. The sergeant lifted the log brace. The gate swung open slightly, and two men came squeezing through with a deer carcass hanging on a pole between them.

They didn't get two feet into the courtyard before the horde fell on the carcass, ripping it to pieces with bare hands and teeth. They ate the whole thing, raw, right there in the courtyard.

Later that day, a Lenape messenger waving a white flag came to the fort. He had a letter from the missionary John Heckewelder. The missionary wrote warning that the Half King Dunquat had demanded that the Lenape help to attack Fort Laurens or the Wyandot would attack the Lenape.

Shortly thereafter, Captain Henry Bird of the British army from Fort Detroit joined Girty to surround the fort. They began a siege to starve out the already starving Americans. Captain Bird was joined by a few British redcoats and one-hundred-eighty native warriors from the Wyandot, Mingo, and Lenape tribes. The British had brought food and plenty of muskets. Black Snake was given a new British musket.

Black Snake had the time of his life. They all did. There was plenty of ammunition so they could shoot again and again. War wasn't so much as killing the enemy, as the whites practiced it, as much as showing how brave one could be. They weren't hitting anything but log walls, but it made a lot of noise, and it was good shooting practice.

They attacked several times, but Captain Bird hadn't brought cannons, which were needed to knock down the palisades. So, militarily, their attacks did nothing. The Indians enjoyed it, though, howling and screaming and shooting the plentiful powder and bullets the British supplied. But it was a cold winter, and the new supply of food the British had brought began to run low.

One night, a volunteer slipped out of the fort at night and made it all the way down to Fort McIntosh with news of the siege. By then, the militiamen had all gone home, and there was just a small Continental force there. Word was forwarded to Fort Pitt.

General McIntosh scrambled to come to their aid. He was unprepared because of the holiday season, and it took three days to get horses packed with barrels of flour. He raced to the rescue. McIntosh also sent a provisioning party under Major Richard Taylor from Fort Pitt all the way down the Ohio River to the Muskingum, with instructions to proceed up the Muskingum, hoping to cross over to the Tuscarawa. His map wasn't accurate, but it contained the best information he had. It looked like Major Taylor could make it, but no one, except Indians and British and French traders, had ever tried that route.

McIntosh himself pushed his soldiers hard, double-time for one-hundred-twenty miles. By the time his reinforcements arrived at the forest outside Fort Laurens, they were exhausted. As they raced towards the protection of the fort, the pack horses stampeded. They ran through the woods in a panic, knocking off the barrels of flour on the trees and scattering the flour throughout the woods.

The British and Indians, though, were gone. They had called off the siege when the leader, Captain Bird, received word that the British Lt. Governor Hamilton had been captured by General George Rogers Clark of the Kentucky militia, farther west at Vincennes. Captain Bird galloped back to Fort Detroit, expecting General Clark to attack there next. The Indians went back home to their warm cabins and wigwams. It was wintertime. Time to be home with family in a warm cabin.

Knotche, Black Snake, and Goose were happy to leave. They headed north. Goose's village wasn't far.

13 LAKE VILLAGE

Knotche and his friends went hungry that first night. Goose and Black Snake set raccoon traps, but even if they worked, there would be no food until morning. To pass the time, they built up a warm fire and played dice games. The trapping was good, though, and they had their fill of raccoons for breakfast. Two days later, they were in Goose's village.

Goose introduced Knotche to his sister. They liked each other right off. Corn Tassel treated Knotche like an honored guest. She had heard stories about Knotche, who her brother referred to as Chief Knotche.

Knotche, unused to the attentions of a woman, was very happy with the situation. On his raiding parties, he rarely smiled. More often, he was grumpy. And lately, it had been even worse. He grieved for his mother, and the winter seemed endless. But once at Goose's village, he was happier than anyone had ever seen him.

Knotche and Corn Tassel spent their days together walking along the lake, talking. At night, Knotche entertained Goose's whole family with the stories he had learned from his father. Everyone lay around the cabin bundled up in furs. The women took turns tending the fire.

Knotche leaned back into Corn Tassel. She wrapped her arms around him to help keep him warm while he spun his yarns. Outside, it was cold and snowing.

"*Long ago,*" Knotche began, "*it is said that an old man lived all alone except for an infant wrapped up in skins. All his relatives and all his nation had been carried off.*

"*He placed the child next to the fire, and after a time, he saw it move. 'Perhaps the little fellow will live,' he said to himself. The child had been left to him.*

"*He made some thin soup of deer's meat and gave it to the little boy. He grew very fast. And the old man made him a bow and arrows.*

"*After a time, the boy asked where his father and mother were, if they hadn't any neighbors. The old man wouldn't tell him.*

"*He waited a while and asked again. The old man said he had had parents and friends but they were killed, but would tell him no more.*

"*The third time he asked, the old man said, 'They have all gone in the direction of the Great Game, ganyo gowa.*

"*But he wouldn't tell what direction that was.*

"*One day, the boy started off thinking he would look for the Great Game.*

"*He came to a small lake, and in the lake was a beautiful swan.*

"*He aimed at the swan and killed it, then he didn't know how to get it as he had no canoe. So he made a line of bark, attached a stone and hook, and threw it beyond where the swan was, and drew it in, a very large swan.*

"*He shook the swan till it was small. Then, taking it on his back, he started home.*

"*When near home, he struck the swan till it was as big as before. Then he said, 'Grandfather, I have got the Great Game.'*

"'*Oh, said the grandfather. 'You shouldn't have killed that swan. It is a harmless bird. You take him right back to the lake and bring him back to life again.'*

"*The boy took back the swan, put it in the water, pushed it off, and said, 'You go off and amuse yourself and live in the water.' The swan swam off alive.*

"*After going back home, the boy insisted on knowing where his parents were, until his grandfather told him he must go off to the east, that it was a six-years' journey for an ordinary man. But a man of power could get there very soon. Halfway was a wizard spring, in which an ugly creature lived. And there his parents and all his friends had perished. He must be careful.*

"*The boy set out, and before noon was at the spring.*

"*When he came to it, he was very thirsty. The water was clear and seemed refreshing. He thought he would drink, but first he would put his foot in the water and see what would happen.*

"*Drawing off one of his moccasins, he put his foot in the water, and the instant he touched it a terrible creature pulled his leg off from the hip and devoured it*

Corn Tassel whispered, "*Oh no!*"

Knotche looked around at his spellbound audience. Goose's uncle, aunt, and mother were all staring at him with a look of shock. Goose and Black Snake smiled. They had heard that part of the story before.

Knotche continued. "*Now, he had but one leg. 'Well,' he thought, 'I'll try again, see if he will pull the other leg off,' and he pulled off his other moccasin. The moment he touched the water, his other leg was pulled off.*

"Now, being without legs, he sat down, pulled hair out of his head, and braided a fishing line, saying 'I'll see if I can catch this creature,' and putting a wooden hook on the line, cut off bits of his flesh and put them on for bait and dropped the hook into the spring.

"It was swallowed immediately, and he jerked a strange creature onto the bank. It was hairy, something like a man, and still like an animal.

"It began to cry piteously. 'Oh, grandson, put me in again.'

"He let the hook down a second time and caught a second creature, a female, which cried like the first. "Oh, grandson, put me in again.'

"'Oh,' said he, 'I can do nothing without my legs. Vomit up my legs.'

"The male vomited up one leg, and then the female vomited up the other. They pushed them towards him.

"He spat on his legs, put them to his body, and was as well as ever.

"Straightening, he gathered a great quantity of dry wood, and set fire to it, saying, 'I can't put you in again. You have destroyed all my friends.'

"He burned them up and went on. As their heads burst, great swarms of mosquitoes came out."

Knotche said, yawning, "There's more to this story. It's a long one. I'll continue another day."

Goose went to see Danelle.

"I'm back!" Goose declared as he ducked through her doorway.

"*What do I care?*" Danelle said. "*I married that trader, Pierre Peltier, who brought me my dream object during the Ononharoia. He's a perfect husband.*"

"*What!? He didn't bring it to you. I chased him down and bought it for you,*" Goose cried.

"Well, thank you," Danelle said and kissed Goose on the cheek. "*He's perfect. Thank you for bringing him into my life.*"

14 HOPOCAN GOES TO WAR

After British Lieutenant-Governor Hamilton was captured by the Kentucky militia led by General George Rogers Clark, the British expected an attack on Fort Detroit, which was weak and undermanned. Arent DePeyster replaced Lt Governor Hamilton. He proposed taking the offensive using His Majesty's Indian allies. A war belt of black wampum was sent out to all the tribes, including, once again, the Lenape.

That winter had been hard for General McIntosh and his soldiers. The soldiers were hungry and ill-clothed, and McIntosh couldn't see a way out of the dilemma he was finding himself in. Somebody on his watch had murdered the leader of a crucial ally. He was expected to make peace with the Indians and capture Fort Detroit with no supplies. And he was expected to rely on the militia. Before he was blamed for failing to do the impossible, General McIntosh requested orders elsewhere - anywhere but Fort Pitt. His request was approved with orders to the south, where he was from.

The Lenape didn't have the luxury of going somewhere else to avoid their difficulties. They, too, were hungry and ill-supplied. They had furs to trade, but the British, though eager to trade with them, insisted the Lenape join with them against the Americans if they wanted to be trading partners. The Lenape needed to buy guns, lead, and gunpowder that they depended upon to hunt for food. The Americans had none of those things to trade.

The Lenape leaders met at the council and discussed their options.

There were basically three factions in Lenape politics. One believed that their best course lay in aligning with the British. The British were primarily interested in trade. They claimed they didn't want native lands like the settlers did. In his Royal Proclamation twenty years earlier, the British King had promised an Indian territory west of the Appalachian Mountains. The British wanted to maintain a mutually beneficial trade relationship with the natives. British manufacturers could trade muskets, woolen blankets, forged knives, axes, pots, and pans for furs. Beaver-skin felt top hats were the fashion rage throughout Europe at a time when all men, and women, too, wore hats. Beaver skins were valuable. So this faction believed that the British only wanted to trade made sense. That was the position adopted by Hopocan.

Another faction, which had been led by Chief White Eyes, believed that the future of his people lay in aligning with the Americans. They could join the American states in an independent but mutually beneficial confederation in much the same way as the Iroquois had done by banding together for power and self-protection. The Americans were doing that now. Chief Killbuck agreed with that position.

A third faction, closely aligned with Chief White Eyes' dream, were the Christian converts. They were convinced that adopting the white man's ways, including his religion, was the path of the future.

Before a decision was made, a delegation of Lenape chiefs, led by Chief Killbuck, White Eyes' successor, traveled to Philadelphia to ask General Washington and the Continental Congress what the Americans' intentions were. At the very least, they needed a partner to trade their furs for the supplies they needed to survive. The Americans had built two forts on their land, Fort McIntosh and Fort Laurens, and neither of them had resulted in a blanket or a lead bullet as a gift, nor was there any trade at all.

Killbuck, along with representatives of the Turkey and Wolf Clans, presented themselves first to General George Washington, who set up his headquarters in Philadelphia when the British had left. The Lenape delegation brought along three boys, as an act of goodwill, to show the Americans that they were sincere in their desire for friendship. They planned to leave the boys with the Americans to be educated in the white man's ways. There was the eight-year-old son of Chief White Eyes, Killbuck's own sixteen-year-old son, and Killbuck's eighteen-year-old half-brother.

Washington was not happy to see them. It was the Continental Congress who made policy, and he didn't want to tell the Indians anything that might depart from Congress' wishes. But Washington was no novice in dealing with Indians in general or the Lenape in particular. He offered the visitors trinkets, tobacco, and whiskey. He told them that their former father, the French King, had agreed to help the Americans fight the British, and the British would soon be defeated. He gave a little speech, dismissed them and sent them over to Congress.

The chiefs got no more satisfaction from the Continental Congress. Congress had rejected the idea of a fourteenth Indian state and had nothing to offer the delegation. They did agree to send the boys to Princeton College. The chiefs returned home with a letter from Congress addressed to Colonel Brodhead, McIntosh's replacement as Commandant of the Western District, directing him to trade with the Lenape if his resources allowed. The delegation stopped at Fort Pitt and presented the letter, but Brodhead had nothing to trade and was trying himself to find, without success, the supplies he needed for his own troops.

When the Lenape delegation arrived back to Coshocton empty-handed, a council was convened, and Hopocan and Killbuck argued their points. Coincidentally, the Wyandot Half King Dunquat sent a messenger to the Lenape demanding that they join with the British or the Wyandot would drive them off their land. The Lenape were living on land claimed by the Wyandot, land that was also claimed by the Iroquois after they had defeated the Huron in the Beaver Wars. The Council voted. This time, many of the chiefs and old warriors sided with Hopocan. Aligning with the Americans had gained them nothing except starvation. Killbuck and a few others who still supported the Americans and refused to alter their stance, fled to Fort Pitt.

Hopocan, war chief of the Lenape, along with many young warriors from his tribe, officially presented themselves at Fort Detroit, where they were welcomed into the fort with a parade. They watched musicians play while the soldiers in their dress uniform of red jackets and white trousers marched in formation around the courtyard performing rifle drills. They twirled around at commands. The butts of muskets banged on the ground in unison, and the muskets were presented "At arms" in snappy precision. The Lenape warriors were fascinated.

Later, a private discussion was held between Hopocan and Governor DePeyster. Hopocan promised to do the British's bidding, and, in return, his warriors would be provided with guns, ammunition, tomahawks, and knives. And, more importantly, British traders would finally be authorized to trade with his tribe.

The Lenape food situation immediately improved now that they had lead and powder to hunt. They could feed themselves.

Hopocan called on all warriors to join him. He sent a message to Goose's village, asking Knotche and his two friends to come with him. Knotche agreed, but he was reluctant to go. He and Corn Tassel had married. Black Snake had gone to Pluggy's Town, and Knotche sent word to him to join them if he was ready for more adventure. Goose, who was broken-hearted with Danelle's rejection, was glad to get away.

Living up to his side of the bargain. Hopocan organized raids on the settlements along the Ohio River. His instruction from Governor DePeyster was to take no prisoners. He was a cagey old war chief. He had not come to his position by accident or inheritance, but by merit. He led several raiding parties himself, composed of Lenape, Mingo, and Ottawa. Warriors set off individually and in bands. They crossed above Fort Henry by canoe, spreading out in different directions. It wasn't a new strategy. The British-aligned tribes had been doing that for years.

Knotche requested that he be allowed to lead a raid inland from Fort Henry to the Wetzel cabin, still intent on taking revenge on the boy whose gun was always loaded, but Hopocan denied the request. He wanted to avoid the strong settlements, like the ones near Fort Pitt and Fort Henry. The raiding parties crossed the Ohio River and harassed settlers north of Fort Henry all the way to Catfish Camp, thirty miles to the north of Wheeling. Knotche led one canoe. He steered his canoe across the current, with Black Snake and Goose, now experienced warriors as well. Along with them were two young Lenape warriors on their first raid. They paddled up the creek the whites called Short Creek.

John Van Metre had already saddled up his horse at first light, planning to head into Beech Bottom for supplies. He was out of coffee. His wife Mary fried him up some corn cakes smothered with fresh butter, eggs, and ham.

The log cabin was small, and the quiet puttering at the fireplace and the whispering of their parents woke fifteen-year-old Hannah and her younger sister Mary. They lay there whispering about the young men they had met at the frolic the previous Sunday. Their three brothers, Isaac, twelve, Abraham, ten, and Johnny, six, lay side by side in their one bed. Isaac awoke. He pulled the covers up over his head, pulling the blanket off his brothers. Abraham grabbed it roughly back and rolled over, pulling the covers off Isaac. Johnny, in the middle, slept through it.

"Can we go with you, Pa?" Hannah asked.

"Yes, can we? Please!" Mary chimed in.

"I need you to do laundry today," their mother said.

Their father wiped his plate with the last of the corn cakes and hurried outside. He didn't like being involved when the girls and their mother clashed.

"Aw, Ma!" Mary pouted. "I feel like a servant around here," Hannah whispered in her sister's ear, and they both giggled.

"I'll ask your father to stay after services on Sunday if you'll get yourselves out of bed and get busy. There's work to be done around here, and I need your help. You can start with that pile of dirty clothes." Their mother pointed to the pile in the corner.

"Aw, Ma." Mary kicked the blanket off them both.

"Your brothers can help you carry the clothes to the spring. You can stay in bed a few minutes longer. There's no hurry. There's a fire going. You can wait until it warms up, dears."

It was late morning when Knotche and his four warriors followed a trail through the woods. They spotted the two teenage girls washing clothes in an open meadow. A hundred yards farther on, they could see the cabin with smoke coming from the chimney. Using hand signals, Knotche ordered the two young Lenape warriors to take the girls while he, Goose, and Black Snake headed back into the woods to circle around closer to the cabin.

Neither of the girls heard or saw a thing. They were both leaning over the shallow pool, working the linen clothing with their hands, talking, when sharp tomahawks came crashing into their skulls. Mary was killed instantly. Hannah was knocked unconscious with a large gash on the top of her head. It wasn't necessary to take all the hair to prove a scalp was taken, but just a handful of hair attached to a patch of skin. The two warriors each took a scalp.

Their mother, hearing a noise outside, stood on a stump chair and looked through the open window towards the barn. It was a high window, built to let in fresh air when the shutters were opened, but high enough so that no one was vulnerable inside the cabin. She didn't see anything. Without thinking, she stepped down from the stump and opened the door to get a better look.

Knotche had told Goose and Black Snake not to fire until he gave the order. They were all startled by the door opening. Without waiting for Knotche's signal, Goose and Black Snake both fired. Both shots hit the woman. One in the forehead and one in the foot. She crumbled to the floor.

Knotche screamed his war cry and rushed to the cabin with his tomahawk raised, not knowing what to expect. He had painted his face completely yellow, and his top-notch was heavily greased. His scream startled Goose and Black Snake, but they quickly recovered, dropped their muskets, and followed him, also yelling their war cries as they pulled out their tomahawks.

Isaac scrambled to the stump and leaped out the window, followed by Johnny. Abraham had been out in the barn feeding the chickens when he heard the shooting and screaming. He hid under a pile of hay. Isaac did a complete summersault and landed on his butt. He took off running. The attackers didn't see him.

Johnny wasn't big enough to leap through the window and was busy pulling himself up when Knotche grabbed him by the leg and pulled him back down.

"Let me go, you fucker!" Johnny yelled, kicking with all his might.

Black Snake grabbed the free leg, and Goose roughly grabbed one arm and the three of them lifted the six-year-old to the rough puncheon floor and flipped him onto his back. Johnny kicked and hit and screamed, and the three warriors laughed, enjoying the struggle, until little Johnny bit Goose on the hand, drawing blood. Knotche knelt on top of the boy and sunk his knee into the boy's chest. Johnny couldn't breathe and quit fighting.

The two warriors with the scalps joined them. They searched the cabin and barn. Clothes, pots and pans, axes, hoes, plus an old musket were loaded up on two of Van Metre's horses. They took their bounty, including young Johnny, back to the river. The horses were swum across while the boy was carried over in the canoe. Hopocan and two scouts were waiting. He congratulated them on their successful raid but questioned Knotche's decision to take the boy prisoner.

"We need boys with spirit," Knotche said.

Black Snake agreed. *"My auntie needs someone to hunt for her."*

Goose shrugged. He had bet them both that Hopocan would kill the boy.

Hopocan agreed to Knotche's request to keep the boy alive. Soon after, more raiding parties returned. Hopocan waited until nearly dark. Not all the raiding parties had returned when they headed inland into the interior of the Ohio country.

Hannah regained consciousness long enough to crawl into the woods and hide under a log. Abraham stayed hidden under the hay, afraid to breathe. Isaac ran all the way to his nearest neighbor, the Staddens. Mortimer Stadden saddled up and rode as fast as he could to Ramsey's Fort. He yelled that there was an Indian attack as he came within sight of the gate and the gate swung open. A company of militia saddled up and rode out, armed and ready. They found the two dead Marys, mother and daughter. Abraham heard the noise, and he crawled out from under the hay. He helped the men look for Johnny and Hannah. They found Hannah, scalped, and unconscious, but still alive. They carried her back to Ramsey's Fort, but she never regained consciousness.

15 LEWIS'S SURPRISE

Sixteen-year-old Lewis Wetzel was a hero to the people on the frontier. He had single-handedly killed two Indians while helping Jacob Sweetwater retrieve his stolen horses. He had killed an Indian who lured two people across the river with a turkey call. And he had rescued Rose Frazier. He was famous for about two weeks after each episode before everyone forgot all about it as they went about their business of staying alive. But everyone knew Lewis Wetzel was special. The children loved him. Adults were starting to think he was a little weird. He had an odd, almost serpent-like way of looking at people.

He continued his night-time forays across the Ohio River into Indian territory, exploring the hills and valleys of the primeval forest, running down the Indian trails at night, just looking to see what he could see. What he always hoped for was to come across an Indian campfire.

Rescuing Rose, he had used the theory he had learned from hearing the stories of the older, more experienced hunters around Wheeling. He was all ears if someone was talking about killing Indians. They said if he could sneak up on a campsite and be sure how many Indians were there, he might be able to kill one or two when they woke in the morning even if there were a bunch. The shouting of "get 'em boys" was part of the theory to get the Indians running scared. He told this theory to Billy Boggs and tried to persuade him to come with him and try it out.

Billy Boggs' reply was, "You're crazy. There is no way in hell I'm getting out of bed to run around all night across the river with you killing injuns. If injuns see us, they'll kill us, or worse. No questions asked."

Billy was the only person Lewis knew he could even ask to go on such a lark. So he went alone. There were no Indian towns anywhere near Wheeling, but as he found out, hunters did come to the woods opposite Wheeling and the island between, occasionally.

One night, he had been exploring down a trail and ran right into a little town of log cabins. It was dark, but he knew it had to be an Indian town since he was on the Indian side of the river. There were no settler towns on that side. Dogs started barking, and he turned and hightailed back out of there as fast as he could. The dogs chased him for a short way but gave up once he was back in the woods. He kept running, just in case.

He wasn't sure where he was, except that he knew he had been heading back towards the river when he spotted the flicker of a campfire not far off the trail. He stopped and rested to catch his breath, leaning on an oak tree as big around as a cabin, before slowly and quietly inching his way closer to the fire.

He saw two Indians sitting around the fire. There was a big roast sizzling over the fire on a spit. Lewis could smell it and his mouth watered. They were talking, but he couldn't understand what they were saying. He slowly backed up, with his rifle ready to shoot, back out to the trail, marking the layout in his mind, noticing the pattern of the trees scattered around so he could find the spot again if the fire was out when he came back.

He counted out a hundred long strides farther down the trail and then walked off the trail on the other side. He lay down next to a fallen tree but couldn't sleep. He went over and over in his head what to do, trying to foresee any difficulties. He prayed for Jesus to give him strength.

Lewis came up with a plan. Shoot one, attack the other with his tomahawk. If he ran, he would chase him, loading as he ran, or if he had to, he would run away and load as he ran. But it had to be light enough so he could see, or he would be at a disadvantage. He had been more confident when somebody was with him like Forrest Frazier had been. He rested awhile, then got impatient, and returned to the Indian camp in the dark. Facing away from the Indian camp, he sat against a big tree and waited.

The night seemed to go on forever. He was hungry and thirsty. He could still smell the cooked meat. It smelled like bear, which he loved. He cursed the Indians. They had food, and he didn't. He finally decided that, since there were only two of them, he could handle it. He would kill them and get something to eat. He silently crept closer. It was still dark, but the eastern sky was lightening up a little. Two Indians were sleeping on the ground, naked except for loincloth and leggings. The fire was out. Moving one foot at a time, rolling from heel to toe carefully and slowly, he inched his way even closer. He gently pulled out his tomahawk, rested his rifle barrel on top of it, and sighted down the barrel at the Indian farthest away.

He said to himself, "Jesus, make my shot run true," as he squeezed the trigger.

BOOM! Fire exploded from the end of the barrel. Lewis leaped at the closest Indian, holding the rifle in one hand and the tomahawk in the other. He shouted, "Get 'em, boys!" He swung the tomahawk just as an old man sat up, catching him right in the forehead. He yanked on the handle and whacked him again and again, but there was no need. The man had been killed with the first blow.

Lewis looked over at the other man when he was suddenly grabbed from behind around the wrist by a firm, strong hand and thrown to the ground. His rifle went flying. He scurried around on hands and knees when a bare foot caught him under the chin, and he went flying over backwards, sending him tumbling over and over. He heard footsteps running down towards him. He scrambled to his feet. A hand grabbed his shirt, and it tore as he took off running as fast as he could, with bushes and branches whacking him in the face and chest.

He had never run so fast in his life. He didn't know how he had escaped. He never even saw who caught him, never saw a glimpse of who it was. Where did that hand come from? Had there been more than two? Whoever it was, was strong. It felt like a vise on his wrist when he was thrown to the ground, and he felt like he was being thrown from a horse. It must have been his grandfather's charm, because it was a miracle he got away. He never let up, never slowed down even when he reached the river. He dove in and swam as fast as he could to the other side.

He collapsed and lay on his back once he reached the Virginia shore, just as the sun rose and the birds started chirping around him. He went over everything in his head. In a flash, he "saw" his mistake. Now, he knew why you don't attack Indians in the dark.

From then on, Lewis never departed from his usual method of waiting until first light when the Indians started waking, then attacking when he was certain of their numbers. He also started dressing more and more like an Indian, even resorting to wearing leggings and loincloth because it made running in the woods more efficient and left nothing to grab on to.

16 RIVER RAIDING

Standing Tree, the Shawnee, had been in Knotche's raiding party when the two Wetzel boys were captured three summers back. He had tracked them to the river after they had escaped, but they had crossed the river to the Virginia side before he got there. Later, Standing Tree had shot a soldier outside Fort Randolph. The fellow militiamen of the fallen soldier had retaliated by murdering the Shawnee Chief Cornstalk and his escort Red Hawk, who were being held prisoner at Fort Randolph. and the chief's son Ellinipsco. With the murder of their chief, the Shawnee had finally accepted the black war belt from Dunquat, which played a role in the capture of Lewis' older brother Martin. Martin Wetzel had been captured by a Shawnee raiding party, patrolling at the request of Dunquat. Martin fought back vigorously and had been adopted into the Shawnee tribe. Given free rein to come and go as he pleased, Martin Wetzel had most of the rights of any other Shawnee warrior but wasn't yet trusted enough to participate in war parties. He stayed behind in Standing Tree's village to help protect it against any attacks, while Standing Tree participated in a large river raiding party.

To stop the horde of white immigrants flooding down the Ohio River, the Shawnee, along with a few Cherokee and Mingo warriors, were using a trick, a ruse. To the Shawnee, all of these whites were trespassing. They hadn't voluntarily relinquished their hunting lands in the Kentuck, the favorite hunting grounds for several tribes. It was thick with game, major sources of protein in their food supply. At first, the immigrants followed Daniel Boone's trail through the Cumberland Gap in the Appalachian Mountains into the buffalo rich Kentuck. Another easier way to bring supplies to Kentucky was by floating down the Ohio River from Fort Pitt. Every day, there were more and more immigrants, like an unstoppable tide. The Shawnee warned the whites at first, and had burned Boone's son as a warning to others, but when that didn't stop them from coming, they waylaid the boats, confiscated everything of value and killed, or took prisoner all on board.

The ruse they used was to direct white children who had been kidnapped and adopted into the Shawnee tribe to stand on the bank of the river and hail ashore travelers heading downriver while warriors waited out of sight. The attacks were conducted at a good spot, too, because just as the big flatboats rounded a point in the river, the boatmen had to quickly maneuver around an island.

These boats were on a one-way journey. They left Fort Pitt loaded down with everything settlers would need in the wilderness and sometimes with several families aboard. The plan for each of them was that the boats would be dismantled and the timber used to build cabins when they reached their destination. Some were fifty-foot keelboats with flat sails to take advantage of any wind. Sometimes, the boats would just be a raft of logs lashed together. They would shove off after rain to take advantage of the high water and fast-moving current. More often, the boats were large flatboats, stoutly made to withstand running aground on sandbars or into logs and trees that fell into the river after rains when the embankments collapsed. These flatboats, or Kentucky boats, up to one-hundred feet long, were covered for protection and to shield the livestock from the sun. They were steered with a large oar in the stern and propelled by both current and at least six men with poles, three on each side.

The river raiding party had been quite successful. That morning, they had captured three different boats when another appeared. Two children adoptees, a boy and a girl, well acclimated to the Shawnee life, were dressed in European clothes captured on a previous raid. They waved to the approaching flatboat.

"Yoo-hoo!" They both called out. "Help us!"

"Where's your parents?" the oarsman called out. The pole men all stopped pushing, but the boat still glided along with the current.

"What?" The boy called out. "I can't hear you."

"Where are your Ma and Pa?"

"Help us please!"

The oarsmen steered the boat in towards shore. It was a cumbersome, forty-foot box of a boat, and it barely turned. He gave instructions to the pole men. They quit poling on one side. The pole-men on the other side pushed hard to turn the boat. One of the men who had quit poling grabbed a musket as a precautionary measure and was loading it when an arrow struck him.

"Back!" Yelled the oarsmen. "Get the hell out of here!" The pole men grabbed for their poles, but it was already too late. Canoes had been launched and were already coming in behind the drifting flatboat. Shawnee, Mingo, and Cherokee warriors leaped aboard, shrieking their war cries. The big flatboat continued to come straight into shore as warriors waded out and leaped aboard.

Standing Tree nimbly ducked under the pole swung at him by one of the pole men. He grabbed it and yanked the man overboard. The man came flying off balance right at Standing Tree with a big splash in waist-deep water. Standing Tree dispatched him with a swing of his tomahawk.

Three men were killed and scalped. Seven other men and women were taken prisoner, as well as three children. Two pigs, a cow, and a dozen chickens were slaughtered and left to rot in the sun. The war party unloaded the settlers' supplies. There were coffee and sugar, hoes and shovels, pots and pans, clothing, blankets, muskets, powder, lead, and even a barrel of rum.

The prisoners were divided up and sent off in different directions, either to be handed over to the British or adopted. The British considered Americans traitors, not prisoners of war, but refrained from hanging them as they would normally have done for treason because of the sympathy that would promote back in Great Britain for the rebel cause. In the east, American traitors were locked in prison camps and on prison ships, where they often died of starvation or disease. In the west, they were sold to farmers and tradesmen, just as the Americans did to British prisoners, to earn their keep. The Shawnee did adopt some and traded prisoners to other tribes as well. There was no prejudice towards them. Once adopted, they were treated like a tribal member, and they often refused to return to the white world if the opportunity presented itself.

As was tradition with the Shawnee, one captive, the oarsman, was painted black and handed a black wampum belt as a warning to other trespassers. They sharpened the end of a pole, stuck it in the ground, and tied the man to it. They piled kindling and dry logs all around it and lit it on fire. The man cried out and begged for his life, but they ignored his pleas.

The captive didn't belong to Standing Tree, and he couldn't interfere, but he could speak his mind. As he had done to save Martin Wetzel's life, he looked around at his fellow warriors and announced, *"We are Shawnee. We do not need to kill defenseless people in our care. I hate these white invaders as much as any of you. But I do not kill unarmed people. That is a cowardly act. I'll have no part in it."* He walked off and refused to participate in any more river raids.

The war party captured several more boats before they disbanded, but they didn't burn any more captives. They were shocked by Standing Tree's words. He had the reputation of being a valiant warrior, and they believed his words were wise.

17 HOPOCAN'S SPEECH

Hopocan of the Wolf clan, war Chief of the Lenape, as well as many others from other clans of the Lenape tribe, had now joined forces with the British. But Hopocan had doubts about his new ally. He didn't trust them. The British had been his enemy during the French and Indian War and had even held him hostage during Pontiac's Rebellion when he presented himself at Fort Pitt under a white flag of truce to parlay.

On his return from one of his war parties on the frontier, Hopocan's doubts about aligning with the British began to reveal themselves when he addressed the British Commandant of Fort Detroit at council. Hopocan spoke English. Also at the council were other British officials, chiefs, and warriors from the British-aligned tribes as well as Catholic and Moravian missionaries. Hopocan had been sent to attack frontier settlements with the specific instructions to take no prisoners. On one raid he personally participated in, he had killed a man and had taken his wife and daughter prisoner. On his return journey, he had handed over the prisoners to the captain of a British ship on the Lakes because the captives slowed his travel.

Chief Hopocan sat in front of the tribal leaders facing the British Commandant, who sat at a long table with other British officials. In Hopocan's left hand, he held a human scalp on a short stick. He rose and addressed the Commandant.

"Father!" Hopocan turned slightly to look at the Indians behind him and said in his own language, *"I call him father, though I don't know why I call him that. I have known no other father than the French. But the British have forced that name on us."* He turned back to the Commandant.

"Father," he continued in English. "You put the tomahawk in my hand and told me to use it on the Long Knives. They had done me no harm. I knew if I didn't obey my father, you would withhold the necessities of life from me, and I had nowhere else to obtain them. You, perhaps, think me a fool to do your bidding. I had no chance of gaining anything. It is your cause, not mine. Many lives have been lost on your account. Children have lost parents, brothers, sisters. Wives have lost husbands. You pretend to hate the Long Knives, but one day you will make peace with them. Who can believe you can love people of a different color better than those who have white skin, like yourselves?"

The Commandant whispered to the official next to him.

"Father! Pay attention to what I am going to say. While you set me on your enemy, much the same way that a hunter sets his dog on game, one day I may look back and see you shaking hands with the Long Knives."

The Commandant gave Hopocan his full attention.

"Now, Father! Here is what I have done with the tomahawk you gave me." He walked forward and handed the stick with the scalp on it to the Commandant. "I have followed your orders. But I did not do all that you ordered. My heart failed me. I felt compassion for your enemy. Women and children have no place in your quarrels. I took captives and am bringing them to you.

"Father! I hope you will not destroy what I have saved. You have the means of preserving that which, with me, would perish from want. The warrior is poor, and his cabin always empty. But your house, Father, is always full. That is all I have to say."*

The Commandant agreed to take in the prisoners. He gave instructions to his aide to contact the ship's captain and see that the prisoners were properly cared for.

"What do you know about spies among your people?" The Commandant asked. "Often, when war parties pass through Delaware territory, our American children are alerted."

Hopocan answered. "Father! That is so. The Long Knives knew I was coming, or I would have taken more scalps. I have long suspected my praying brothers. They have adopted the white man's ways, and that is part of it."

"Or their teachers?"

"Yes, Father. Perhaps."

The Commandant whispered to his aide.
After Hopocan spoke, the Wyandot Chief Tarhe gave his report.

* For Hopocan's entire speech, see page 133 of <u>History, Manners and Customs of the Indian Nations,</u> John Heckewelder.
Heckewelder dates this speech by Captain Pipe (Hopocan) Dec. 9, 1801. Other sources show he was dead by then, so I've used it here

18 BROADHEAD

Four of the Iroquois's six nations had joined with the British forces against Washington's army in the east. The following spring, General Washington finally had the men and resources he needed to embark on an Indian campaign. His order to his generals was to not merely overrun the Iroquois towns in New York and Pennsylvania but to destroy them. Burn the houses and torch the food supply. He directed his generals not to listen to any overtures of peace until the Indian towns lay in ruins.

Colonel Brodhead wrote to Washington and asked for permission for an ambitious western campaign, too. He could attack the Seneca, one of the warring Iroquois Nation tribes, from the west. Afterwards, he proposed, he would attack the Delaware towns and then drop down the Scioto River to take out the Shawnee, leaving the Ohio country wide open. Then, he could advance unmolested upon and destroy the British at Fort Detroit.

Brodhead was born in New York and had been raised in Pennsylvania. As a boy, his family home had been attacked by native war parties numerous times during the French and Indian War and Pontiac's Rebellion afterwards. Washington got to know him well at the Battle of Long Island as well as the winter they spent together at Valley Forge. Broadhead had frontier war experience, too, having served under General McIntosh for a year.

While Brodhead waited for Washington's response, he used his limited supplies the best way he could. He sent provisions to Fort Laurens and withdrew the regulars from Fort Randolph. As soon as the army pulled out of Fort Randolph, the Shawnee burned it to the ground.

Washington at first denied Brodhead's request. He ordered Brodhead to remain at Fort Pitt to protect the surrounding country. Washington was concerned that if the troops left the area, it would invite Indian attacks. He also couldn't get supplies to the western outpost in a timely manner for Brodhead to conduct a campaign against the Seneca at the same time that General Sullivan was leading the army to attack the Iroquois from the east.

But as Sullivan's campaign advanced successfully, burning Iroquois towns and crops, Washington finally had the support and resources he needed, and he approved Brodhead's request for a campaign up the Allegheny River to attack the Seneca towns. Funds were supplied. Washington envisioned the two forces, General Sullivan's and Colonel Brodhead's, meeting and then capturing the British Fort Niagara. He instructed Brodhead to bring only light artillery so he could move quickly.

Brodhead sent notices requesting volunteers. Few in Wheeling were interested, but for the settlers closer to Fort Pitt, who were often attacked by the Seneca, men signed up in sufficient numbers to make a fairly large force. Some of the Lenape were still loyal to White Eyes and now Chief Killbuck. They also offered to help.

Brodhead put together an army of six-hundred and five soldiers, Continentals as well as militia. He sent supplies upriver by boat as far as Mahoning. From there, the supplies were loaded on two-hundred packhorses and proceeded upriver. An advance guard of fifteen soldiers and eight Lenape warriors led the way.

There was little resistance to Brodhead's Seneca Campaign up the Allegheny River. Most warriors had headed east to fight General Sullivan's forces, leaving their villages undefended. He burned ten villages. Including scalp bounties offered by Pennsylvania's government and the plunder collected, his men carried off thirty-thousand dollars' worth of treasure to divide up among themselves.

Colonel Brodhead planned to do the same thing to the Delaware that he'd done to the Seneca - burn their towns and crops. The Delaware were split in their loyalties. Most had joined with Hopocan and were doing the bidding of the British by attacking the frontier settlements. The Moravians did their upmost to stay out of the conflict, taking the path of peace. Only a few remained loyal to the faction led by Chief Killbuck. Killbuck's warriors who aided the Americans in the Seneca campaign were glad they did. They were on the winning side. To honor Colonel Brodhead, they gave him an Indian name, *Machinque Keesuch* (Great Moon), and made him a chief. Chief Great Moon sent out word to all the tribes inviting them to align with the Americans. Many tribes, including the Chippewa on Lake Superior and the Cherokee in Tennessee, responded favorably, seeing the tide of war turning against them. Even the Wyandot Half King Dunquat came to Fort Pitt to meet with Chief Great Moon, willing to discuss peace.

Chief Killbuck provided intelligence to Brodhead. He told him that the Lenape villages were largely undefended as most of the chiefs and warriors, including the war chief Hopocan, were at Fort Detroit or on raiding parties. He told Brodhead of the vulnerabilities of the Lenape towns and even offered to lead the American army against them himself.

It was difficult, however, for Colonel Brodhead to raise the necessary troops and supplies for another campaign because both he and General George Rogers Clark, the young Kentucky hero with success at his back after capturing the British Lt. Governor Hamilton, were competing for the same men and supplies on the western frontier. Clark already had the backing of the Virginia Governor. Brodhead needed Washington's support. June turned into July, which became August, then September, and still, no supplies were available for either of their campaigns, and the season to go on the offensive was ending. The campaigns were postponed.

By spring, things changed. Lenape war parties, led by Hopocan himself, were again taking prisoners and scalps on the frontier.

Unexpectedly, Brodhead received funds authorizing him to pay bonuses for new recruits. Instead of using the funds for that designated purpose, he used the money to outfit his campaign and hurried downriver on flatboats with one-hundred-fifty Continentals. He sent a canoe ahead to Colonel David Shepherd at Fort Henry, requesting volunteers as soon as possible.

When Colonel Brodhead and his men poled their boats into the landing at Wheeling, the whole town showed up to greet them. Brodhead was the first Commandant of the Western District who had actually defeated Indians. Hand had been a laughing stock after his Squaw Campaign. One of his officers had allowed the murder of the respected Shawnee chief Cornstalk by militiamen. McIntosh had built forts but had turned the Delaware against them after the murder of Chief White Eyes. The settlers' only defense against Indian attacks were their forts, stockades and blockhouses, and Indian fighters like Lewis Wetzel. Brodhead was their champion for wiping out the Seneca towns. Everyone that went along on the Allegheny excursion not only came back, except one man who had drown, but they had come back well-compensated for their service. Colonel Brodhead had their respect.

Respect wasn't enough, however. There wasn't a lot of interest in joining Colonel Brodhead's regulars. Leaving their homes unprotected was always risky. The young hero of Wheeling, Lewis Wetzel, helped tilt the balance in Brodhead's favor.

Billy Boggs and Lewis were standing around, looking at the poster as it was read aloud.

"Wanna go?" asked Billy. "That last one old Brodhead went on made everybody rich."

Lewis looked up at the sky. Clouds were gathering from the south, and the sky was darkening, though it was only midday.

"Yeah, maybe," Lewis said. He liked the idea of an expedition that had the expressed goal of killing Indians. His last army experience, helping build Fort McIntosh, hadn't been so bad. He'd made twenty dollars. But Indian hunting was terrible. He knew a large army wouldn't get ten feet into Indian territory without the Indians knowing about it unless the weather turned bad. Lewis had always found that bad weather was a good time to move through the woods undetected. If it was bitterly cold or raining, chances were good that any natives would be holed up somewhere staying warm and dry. To Lewis' way of thinking, bad weather was a good time to kill Indians.

Those two words, "Yeah, maybe," spread quickly throughout the Wheeling settlement. When they heard that Lewis Wetzel was thinking about putting his X on the enrollment list, the volunteers started lining up. With the bold young hero Lewis Wetzel along, the chances of bringing back their own scalps intact, many figured, and Indians scalps, too, increased dramatically.

Lewis' X, though, had the opposite effect on some of the older men. Lewis Wetzel, and his brothers and father, too, had the reputation of being impulsive hotheads that could get them into trouble. It was the young men who joined in numbers.

As the day approached for the campaign against the Delaware to begin, the troops were drilling, and the officers were coordinating supplies on the flatboats, and recruiters were still signing up militiamen. Two Indians crossed the river and brazenly walked up to the Fort holding their palms up in the sign of peace and waving a white flag. They asked to meet with Colonel Brodhead. They told him they had been sent by Chief Killbuck to help guide Brodhead's army to Coshocton. Killbuck himself, they told him, would join them on the trail.

Lewis had been talking with his brother Jacob down by the river when the two Lenape crossed over. Lewis had considered shooting them on the spot, and would have if he'd had his musket with him. Instead, he was supposed to be on latrine duty and had left his rifle in the militia tent. He said to his brother, "That's one of the varmints that took us, Jacob. I'd know him anywhere."

"The one with the hooked nose? Naw, that don't look nothing like him," Jacob replied.

"Look at that nose ring! That's the only difference!" Lewis countered. "That's him! I'd recognize him anywhere."

The man he was referring to was Coopeeconain, a second cousin to Knotche on his mother's side. He was from the Moravian village of Lichtenau and a devout Christian.

That night, Brodhead gave orders that the army would leave promptly after muster in the morning. Colonel David Shepherd would lead the militiamen. The plan was to march up the river trail and cross over at the shallow ford where they could pick up the Old Mingo Trail to Coshocton. That night, because of the universal hatred in and around Wheeling for all Indians, one of Brodhead's officers suggested that the two Indian guides sleep in the guardhouse for their own safety. Brodhead ordered it done.

Lewis and Billy decided, as a lark, to get an early start on killing Indians. Nobody expected any trouble with this many armed men, so there were few guards on duty. They waited until everyone was asleep except the watches. Their buddy Daniel Greathouse agreed to keep the guardhouse sentry preoccupied with a game of pinochle. There was no lock or key on the guardhouse, just a crossbar to keep someone in the room from getting out.

A summer storm made Lewis' and Billy's "lark" easy. There was lightning close by. The lightning struck with a loud THWACK. Six seconds went by before another THWACK. Then the low rumble of thunder. The rain poured.

The two quietly lifted the crossbar. The two sleeping Lenape guides didn't see or hear a thing. Coopeeconain was an older man, the other, a young teenage relative of Chief Killbuck. Lewis took the older man, the one he was sure was Knotche. Billy took the boy. They had pre-arranged a signal - Lewis would show one finger, then two, and on the count of three, they would strike together. There was no outcry. Just a near-simultaneous dull thump as the Indians' heads were split open. Billy wiped his tomahawk clean on the dead boy's shirt. Lewis couldn't get the blade of his out because it was buried so deep. They didn't bother to take scalps, knowing that it could be trouble to be caught with them. They tiptoed back out, waved to Greathouse, and turned in for the night.

In the morning, the troops were mustered. There were 134 militia volunteers, including Billy and Lewis, along with the Continentals from Fort Pitt.

Brodhead was anxious to get moving as more rain was expected, which would make it difficult to cross the Ohio River. He was giving orders to send flatboats and every other floating contraption he could find up ahead to meet the men at the crossing when one of his aides informed him of the two dead Lenape guides.

Brodhead was furious. He had all the men muster. He held up the tomahawk left in Coopeeconain's skull in front of the soldiers and demanded to know who owned it.

Nobody answered. It was a distinctive tomahawk with its carved snake twining up the handle. Many recognized it. It was the one Lewis had found stuck in his family's cabin door. Lewis was proud of it and had shown it off frequently. But nobody spoke up.

Rather than delay his campaign, Colonel Brodhead set out immediately. He figured that the loss of the guides wouldn't affect his operations. Chief Killbuck had already drawn him a map and was supposed to meet him. He didn't ignore the murders, though. He left the distinctive tomahawk behind with Colonel Ebenezer Zane as evidence. Zane stayed behind with a skeleton crew of militiamen to guard the fort while the Commander of the fort, Colonel Shepherd, led the expedition's   militia.

19 GNADENHUTTEN

The army marched upriver to the ford without any major problems. The current was strong with the rainfall, so they had to cross a little farther upstream than Killbuck's map indicated. They landed in the backwater current just below the old Mingo village where the trail started.

They took off at a fast march with a squad of scouts riding ahead. The rain started gently at first, and it kept the air cool and refreshing, but by noon, it had turned into a torrential downpour. The Indian trail was muddy and slippery at first, then turned into a glue-like goo. The officers' and scouts' horses had to be walked so they wouldn't get injured. To many of the militia, who lived and hunted every day in this weather, it was no big deal. The rain was warm, almost tropical, and it kept the wretched mosquitoes away. It was the Indians they worried about. Indian raids had been frequent enough, and the atrocities severe enough, that most of them were jittery being in Indian territory. Every one of them had been affected in one way or another, whether it was a friend or relative scalped or taken prisoner or had personally fought a life and death struggle against a native foe. Lewis wasn't worried at all. He knew the Indians would be home in their dry huts and cabins.

The hunters in the group showed the others, when they stopped for the night, how to make a quick, dry shelter from sticks and leaves and how to build a fire by splitting open a log and shaving off plenty of dry kindling. It took a hot fire to get wet wood to burn.

Colonel Brodhead sent a scout ahead to the Delaware Moravian town of Salem, where the missionary spy John Heckewelder lived. "Tell him it's urgent, that he come right away," Brodhead told the scout Sam Brady.

Heckewelder, with a couple of young Lenape men as escorts, arrived at the soldiers' wet camp the next morning. Colonel Brodhead thanked him for coming on such short notice. He asked the missionary to warn any peaceful Delaware who might be in the area hunting to stay clear of his army lest they be mistaken for the enemy by his trigger-happy militia. He was concerned that any Christian Indians would be killed before they could identify themselves as non-combatants. He also asked if there was a safe, dry place where his men could rest before their operations.

Heckewelder told Brodhead about the Moravian village of Gnadenhutten. Brodhead could get food and shelter there. He wrote a note in German for the missionary at Gnadenhutten, David Zeisberger, and sent the note on ahead with one of his escorts.

As the army slogged up the trail through the woods towards the Tuscarawa River, Colonel Shepherd, the militia commander, stopped occasionally and waited under trees and counted the men to make sure they were all present and accounted for. He knew desertion was common with militiamen the closer they got to Indians.

Shepherd had as much reason to hate Indians as anyone there. His son William and son-in-law Francis Duke had been killed by Indians when the Half King

Dunquat had led the attack on Fort Henry two years before. He also knew his militiamen could, and would, take matters into their own hands if they thought they could get away with it. Sometimes, it was hard to tell what they'd do if they saw Indians. They might shoot them, or they might run. They were afraid of Indians, and had good reason to be. Shepherd had been commanding the militia for years, and as Sheriff of Ohio County, little got by him. He was a good sheriff. He knew what these men were capable of, and he kept an eye out for trouble.

He asked the last man in the column, Jason McCollough, where everybody else was. McCullough just shrugged his shoulders. Shepherd saw the flick of McCollough's eyes as he unconsciously glanced into the woods to the north.

"Gol-darnit!" Shepherd muttered. He galloped ahead and informed Brodhead. Then he took off back down the trail, slapping his horse with the reins.

The trail wasn't hard to follow. A hundred yards back, a new trail led off into the woods. He found a dozen men sitting under a big maple, smoking pipes.

Lewis had known the trail the army was on led to a Moravian village, but he also knew a shorter way to get there. He had suggested to some of the other militiamen that if they fell behind, they could then make a dash across the ridges and kill as many Indians as they wanted.

"Easy pickings," he told them. "They won't even fight back."

Shepherd rode into the middle of them. "Best you boys catch up," Shepherd said, looking straight at

Lewis. "Ain't safe in these woods. Best we stick together."

Nobody moved, and they all looked to Lewis.

"Not in a while, boys. Now. That's an order. Move." Shepherd was the age of most of their fathers, and his face got hard, his voice menacingly low. "Wetzel, I want you to join Brady up front, as scout."

Lewis smiled his big white toothy engaging grin, but he couldn't hide the black, hard, serpent-like eyes.

"Got that?" Shepherd repeated.

"Yes, sir," Lewis mumbled. Lewis knocked his tomahawk pipe against the tree, and the burning ashes fell to the ground with a sizzle and went out. He slipped the pipe into the empty sheath on his right hip, then stood up, stretching. The others did the same.

Shepherd told Brodhead that the militia shouldn't be trusted in this village overnight if he didn't want trouble. There was no telling what they'd do.

Colonel Brodhead was an experienced combat officer. He always looked out for the welfare of the men under his command. Now, he needed his men to be rested and ready to fight. Sleeping out of the rain, in some place dry, was a necessity. He mustered the men just outside the village of Gnadenhutten.

"These people are not our enemies," Brodhead told them. "If the hair on one head is disturbed in any way, we'll be having target practice on the perpetrators in the morning. Do I make myself clear?"

Nobody said anything. The men fidgeted and shifted their weight, and looked around at the others.

"What does perp-a-tater mean?" Lewis whispered to Billy.

"It means we can't kill any of these Indians," Billy said, "Or that bastard will have us shot."

"Do I make myself clear?" Brodhead said again, raising his voice.

"Yes, sir!" Everyone shouted.

The people of Gnadenhutten welcomed the troops to their pleasant, well laid out village with wide roads, log cabins, and a church at the center. The bell in the church steeple rang as they entered the village, and the people lined the streets. In one of the barns, a feast was laid out for them out of the rain. There were hams, apples, corn, and fresh milk. The officers' horses were bedded down and fed fresh hay and corn in a separate barn. After the meal, the officers were escorted to houses, and beds of hay were laid out for the soldiers in another of the dry barns.

Brodhead visited the soldiers before turning in. He had them fall in. The regulars stood in line at attention. The militiamen stood slouched, hands in pockets if they had them, leaning on one leg, relaxed, some smoking pipes. As he walked down the line, he said, "We're guests of these people. I want them treated with respect. Any of these people get hurt by any of you, I'll shoot you myself. Is that clear?"

There was no answer.

"What about sparking?" asked Billy, "I mean, if they're willing." That brought a laugh from everyone. Even Brodhead tried not to show his smile.

Colonel Brodhead walked over to Billy.

"What's your name, son?" He asked.

"Boggs, sir. William Boggs."

"You think this is funny, Private Boggs? These people are putting us up, feeding us, with some danger to themselves, and you want to have sex with their daughters? These people are Christians, Boggs, just like us."

"Christians mate, sir! Ain't you noticed?"

The barn filled with laughter.

"Keep your trousers on, Private Boggs." He stepped back and addressed all of them. "That goes for everybody."

For most of the troops, the stop in Gnadenhutten was a civilized break from bad weather, and they would have been perfectly happy to lounge there until the rain quit. But Colonel Shepherd was anxious to get his militiamen far away from the peaceful Moravians, and Colonel Brodhead was anxious to attack the Lenape capital while the warriors were away as his intelligence had suggested.

That night, led by the missionary David Zeisberger, the entire Christian congregation gathered at the barn and sang hymns to the soldiers. Afterwards, Lewis exclaimed, "I got to get away from the stink of these savages."

In a dry cabin, Colonel Brodhead laid out his plans for Colonel Shepherd. Coshocton consisted of one-hundred log cabins and bark shacks spread out for a mile along the river. They would attack from three sides, trapping the Indians at the river. They would divide the force into three, with a prearranged time to swoop in. The north and south forces would make a wide arc around the village to catch the Indians by surprise. The force attacking from the east would keep anyone from escaping, pinned against the river.

In the morning, the army headed out after eating fresh bread and hot coffee made and served by the Moravians. It was still raining.

Chief Killbuck, with a small band of Lenape warriors loyal to him, caught up with the army as they headed towards Coshocton. He didn't ask about the two scouts he'd sent, and no one volunteered the information that they'd been murdered. He led the army through the forest, bypassing the small village called White Eyes' Town .

20 DEFEAT

Coshocton was largely undefended as Brodhead had hoped. Most of the Delaware warriors were gone. At that very moment, they were out on raiding parties. Colonel Brodhead put his three-pronged attack into motion but ended up, with Killbuck's help, capturing the entire town without a shot.

All the cabins and wigwams were searched for anything of value before they were torched. There was a large amount of bundled furs ready for sale and a few muskets. They filled Colonel Brodhead's travel chest with silver jewelry. There wasn't a lot of livestock, but the traditional natives were beginning to appreciate the advantages of their Moravian brethren. Cattle, pigs, chickens, and ducks were slaughtered, and the cornfields and grain storage bins were burned. The Lenape horses were loaded with plunder.

As was often the case when Continentals teamed up with militiamen, the troops asked if they could vote on what to do with the captives. In the new world of American freedom and democracy, every man's voice was as important as any other. The militia had voted on who their officers would be, and they wanted to vote on when the expedition was ready to return home, too. Colonel Brodhead gave his consent to a democratic vote.

The prisoners' fate was quickly decided with a unanimous decision. The warriors - sixteen of the villagers were young men, so were considered warriors - were given the death penalty. The others, old men, women, and children, would be brought back to Fort Henry. The militiamen volunteered to do the executions.

The young Lenape men, with their hands tied behind them with rawhide, were escorted to the edge of the smoldering cornfield. The militiamen drew straws to see who got to be executioners. Both Billy and Lewis drew a short straw. The warriors were turned to face the cornfield, away from the executioners. At the count of three, Brodhead shouted, "Let her rip!"

Lewis, Billy, and the other selected militiamen sunk their tomahawks into the skulls of the young Delaware men. Then throats were slit, scalps taken.

That night, across the river, there was screaming and yelling around a bonfire loud enough to wake snakes. A young captive told them it was a war party that had returned from a successful raid. They were drinking whiskey and dancing around a bonfire. Brodhead ordered the men to find some canoes. They would cross the river and attack.

One of the militiamen spoke up, "No way to get over there, sir. The river's swollen, and them injuns took all the canoes."

Broadhead turned to Shepherd. "Any suggestions?"

"We could knock together a few rafts. Or we could send someone back to Gnadenhutten. They've got canoes."

139

However, the men, after traveling for days through mud and rain and now had scalps, were not eager to cross the river to attack someone who might fight back.

"Let's go get another town," said one Private. "We don't need to go against a bunch of crazy, drunk injuns. That'd be nuts."

Another shouted out, "Let's vote on it."

Brodhead again authorized a vote, and the militiamen and some of the Continentals applauded with a loud "Hurrah!"

"This is what democracy is all about," said another private.

They voted to ignore the Indians across the river and unanimously agreed to head home in the morning.

Chief Killbuck informed Colonel Brodhead that he would take care of the drunk Lenape warriors himself. He rode off upriver with the four warriors who had come with him.

The next morning, the army was hailed from the other side of the river. Three older men stood there on the opposite shore.

"We want to talk to your Chief." The army translator and scout Montour told Colonel Brodhead.

"What do they want?" Brodhead asked. Montour translated.

"We want to talk peace," was the reply.

"Through the translator, Brodhead said, *"Come over. We will talk peace."*

"Maybe not safe," was the reply.

"You have my word," Brodhead said. *"You can cross safely, and I will protect you."*

A few minutes later, one older man, a Lenape Chief, pushed off in a canoe. The current was strong, and the canoe took him farther downstream, past where Brodhead waited, around a bend in the stream. Lewis Wetzel had been watching what was going on and ran over to where the canoe was sure to land, taking into consideration the current.

As the Chief beached his canoe, Lewis reached out with one hand to take the man's hand. With the other, he swung his tomahawk pipe down on the man's head.

When Brodhead got there, Lewis was gone, and the scalped Chief was already floating face down in the fast-flowing river.

"Who the blazes did that, gol-darnit!" barked Brodhead. No one knew.

The rain stopped, and the sun came out. The mud started to dry up, and the air was thick and muggy and full of ravenous mosquitoes. Brodhead ordered the army to head home. They stopped to use the spring at another small Lenape town, Newcomer's Town, giving the officers a chance to water their horses. While they were resting, Chief Killbuck caught up to them. He and his warriors had crossed the river and attacked the drunk Lenape warriors as he'd promised. He threw a scalp at Colonel Brodhead's feet. "Him very bad."

The expedition was a success as far as defeating the Lenape, but word of the fiasco filtered back to General Washington from subordinates of Brodhead. Washington's friend William Crawford told of the young Delaware men ruthlessly killed by the militia under Brodhead's command and questioned whether it was even necessary to destroy a tribe that had once been friendly to the United States. The auditor of the Western District circulated a petition for Brodhead's removal based on his misuse of recruiting funds to pay for the expedition against Coshocton. Washington wrote to Brodhead and suggested that he resign his position until the matter could be investigated. Brodhead refused and demanded a court-martial to prove his innocence.

21 THE MORAVIANS

A few days later, eighty Shawnee and Lenape warriors, led by the Lenape War Chief Buckongahelas, surrounded the Moravian village of Gnadenhutten and demanded the Christians hand over the traitor Chief Killbuck. Buckonghelas was an older man, older than Hopocan. He had fought alongside the French in the French and Indian War. He had grown up across the Ohio River in Virginia. White settlers had killed his son there, and he had spent nine years tracking down and taking his revenge on the murderer. Buckongahelas, after he received word of the attack by Brodhead on the Lenape capital of Coshocton with the help of Killbuck, moved his family north to live near his friend and ally, the Shawnee Chief Blue Jacket, who had himself joined his relatives, the Miami, in the northwest part of the Ohio country.

The Moravian leader Isaac told Buckongahelas' large party of warriors that Chief Killbuck was no longer in the area but was now living at Fort Pitt. Buckongahelas ordered the town searched. The warriors looked through all the stables, barns, cabins, and root cellars. Buckongahelas then ordered that the leaders of all the Moravian villages be sent for. When they arrived, he addressed them.

"Friends and Kinsmen! Listen to what I say to you! We are a great and powerful nation divided! At first, I saw the fight between the British and the Americans as a fight between father and son, and I was not interested.

However, after a time, it appears the father was in the right, and the children deserve to be punished - a little. I decided that after I saw the cruel acts the American children have committed on us. They've taken our lands, stolen our property, shooting and murdering our men, women, and children.

"Friends and relatives! Now listen to me and hear what I have to say to you. I've come to bid you to go with me to a secure place. Do not covet the land you now cultivate. I will take you to a country equally as good where your fields shall yield abundant crops, where your cattle will find good pasture and where there is plenty of game, where your women and children and yourselves will live in peace and safety and where no Long Knives shall ever molest you. I will live between you and them to protect you. There, you can worship your God without fear. If you stay where you are now, one day, the Long Knives will, in their usual way, speak fine words, and at the same time murder you."

After taking a break to discuss what Buckongahelas had said, the Moravians gathered again. Isaac addressed Buckongahelas and the warriors.

"Friends and Relatives! Thank you for your well-meaning talk. We're sorry to learn that you have such a bad opinion of our white brothers, the Americans, who have sprung from the same soil as us. We have found no reason to distrust the Americans, and as we have never committed a hostile act against the Americans, we have no reason to fear injury from them. If you, our friends and relatives, love us, you should avoid our peaceful settlements when you go out to commit hostilities, or when returning from them. Nothing draws the enemy upon us sooner than you making war paths through our

settlements. Now, we have too much property to think of pulling it all up and going with you."

Buckongahelas replied, "Your words proceed from a good heart, a heart which can't think bad of anyone. However, the Long Knives will always remain the same until they have got all our land from us.

"At first, when I spoke to you, I did not intend to compel you. I had no intention to make you leave your settlement, but only to warn you of the danger of living here. Now, I say to you, my friends and relatives, let everyone among you exercise his free will, either to go or to stay. Don't try to stop anyone who wants to leave to go to a safe place."*

The gathering broke up, with everyone agreeing to consider Buckongahelas' proposal. The leaders returned to their villages. Buckongahelas and his warriors then proceeded to the Moravian village of Salem. Buckongahelas wanted to meet with the missionary John Heckewelder. A runner was sent ahead to ask the villagers to provide them a reception.

Heckewelder thanked Buckongahelas for his concern and the trouble he had taken to inform them of their danger. "We will trust in the Lord," the missionary told him. "He is our shepherd. We are his sheep."

A few of the Moravians agreed to leave with Buckongahelas, but most stayed. They, like their pastor Heckewelder, trusted God to protect them.

That wasn't the last of it, however. Governor DePeyster then sent another delegation to the Moravians. This time, they didn't politely ask them to leave.

145

* For Buckongahelas' entire speech, see page 216, <u>A Narrative of the Mission of the United Brethren Among the Delaware and Mohegan Indians</u>, by Johann Heckewelder

22 PANDEMONIUM

The Wyandot Half King Dunquat was given the task of moving the Moravians, by force if necessary. Hopocan assisted. The trader Matthew Elliot, who had accompanied Simon Girty and Alexander McKee when they had deserted from Fort Pitt, joined Dunquat's band at Fort Detroit. Knotche and Black Snake joined Hopocan. Goose fell in with the Wyandot chiefs and warriors. The Shawnee Standing Tree, Knotche's, Goose's, and Black Snake's old friend from their first raiding party together in which they had kidnapped the two Wetzel boys, came riding up with a band of Shawnee led by chiefs John and Thomas Snake, to assist.

The old friends dismounted and greeted each other warmly.

"May you be in a good frame of mind and good health."

It's good to see you, my friend."

"Where have you been?"

Standing Tree stood stoically, with his head held high, dressed impeccably, with fresh deerskin leggings, clean blue loincloth and a white linen shirt. He was shorter than all of them, but he held himself erect and proud. He appeared a little awkward from the attention.

"You didn't catch those boys, did you?" Black Snake asked.

147

"How did you know?" Standing Tree replied, looking the Mingo Black Snake over from head to foot like he was seeing him for the first time. Black Snake had lines on his face, and there were bags under his eyes. The last they'd seen each other was three years before, and they'd all led hard lives since then. Black Snake's hair was the same as last they'd seen each other, still in a Mohawk. The Shawnee was still wearing his in a top-notch gaily decorated with red ribbons and feathers. He, too, seemed weary.

Goose said. *"We saw that older boy, the wounded one. He killed two of my friends."*

"That's right," added Knotche. *"I led a party into the Land of the Skull for horses. We got two handfuls."* He flashed all nine fingers – twice. *"Nice horses. We crossed back over the river with them."*

Standing Tree stood quietly. He nodded.

"Well, he has a gun that is always loaded," Black Snake added.

"Yes," said Knotche, *". . . and he stopped us. We tried to take our revenge, too, but the Spirit smiles on him."*

"He took all our horses, too," said Black Snake.

Standing Tree lifted his chin slightly, urging him to tell more,

"And killed two friends of mine," Goose said. *"The Spirit looks out for him. He has magical powers."*

"Those were smart boys. They would have made good warriors," said Standing Tree. *"I did my best to catch them, but they had already crossed back over the river by the time I got there."*

"Hey!" Said Black Snake. *"We had a bet on that. I think you owe me, Knotche."*

"*No, you owe me,*" he said. "*I think. It's been a long time. Are you sure?*"

They camped outside Gnadenhutten, and word was sent to the Moravians to come listen to Half King Dunquat speak. Everyone was required to come, everyone was to be accounted for, by order of Dunquat. While they waited for the Moravians' arrival, Dunquat instructed his warriors to leave the Moravian converts and their property in peace, at least for now.

Once assembled, Dunquat told the Moravians, "*For a long, time I have been concerned on account of my cousins, the Christians, living in such a dangerous place - between two powerful, angry armies. It is not advisable to remain. You will perish - women and children, too, if you remain. I want to take you by the hand and lead you to safety. You will find plenty of provisions where I will take you. Plus, your Father, the British Governor at Detroit, will also provide for you.*"

Isaac, representing the Moravians, replied, "*We are at peace with all mankind. We have nothing to do with war. No one will hurt us. We wish to remain where we are. Besides, we have too much property to go - but we will consider your offer and give you our answer in the spring.*"

Dunquat, as he had in the past, accepted that reply and agreed that it would be wrong to move the Moravians from their favorite spots where they were happy and content.

The trader Matthew Elliot had received personal instructions from Lt. Governor DePeyster that the Moravians were to be rounded up and removed. No excuses. Elliot demanded that Dunquat and Hopocan not give up so easily, as Buckongahelas had done just days before, and threatened to tell DePeyster that they were not following the Governor's directive. He told Dunquat that all the Moravians had to be moved to ensure the problem of someone spying on British and Indian movements was eliminated.

Dunquat assented.

The tribal leaders, though, were divided over what to do with the converts and missionaries. The Wyandot warriors believed they should protect the Moravians but wanted to scalp the missionaries. The Lenape warriors believed the missionaries were good, wise people. They were leaders in tribal affairs and had helped their people. They shouldn't be killed. The Shawnee wanted to use this large force to attack their enemies in the Kentuck land. To them, the Moravians were always cooperative and helpful whenever they were asked, and so no reason to harm any of them.

Suddenly, someone let out a scalp yell, and everyone grabbed their muskets in readiness. The Wyandot warriors thought it was time to kill the Christian teachers. Knotche was confused. Black Snake looked to Knotche for direction. Knotche looked to Hopocan. Hopocan looked to Dunquat. Knotche expected the Moravians, led by Isaac, who had once been a war chief, to attempt to rescue their teachers. Would he be expected to shoot them, people he was related to, even if he didn't know them, except Isaac, personally? He was a Munsee, part of the Lenape tribe. Even though he had led raiding parties back through Lenape territory, it was only to force them to join the war, not to hurt them.

Warriors were running everywhere, with no one directing. It was total confusion. Some wanted to start killing. The Lenape tried to shield the Moravian converts, with the missionaries in their midst. They didn't try to stop the Wyandots when they grabbed the missionaries. The converts also did nothing to stop them. The Shawnee watched.

The Wyandots stripped the missionaries of their black suits. They took their shoes, buckles and cut off the buttons from their clothes.

A Wyandot warrior grabbed each missionary by the hair and shook them one by one. With each shake, he said, *"Quawongomel Nimat!"* - *"I salute thee, my brother!"* He then turned to Heckewelder and yanked the linen shirt from him, tearing it off his back, saying, *"Friend, I am in want of a shirt, and I must have yours!"*

Standing Tree stepped up and pushed the Wyandot, who was a head taller than him. *"Coward! Be gone! What harm have these people done you? You are always foremost where there is no danger!"* That warrior, stunned by the rebuke, meekly drifted into the crowd with the torn shirt.

Reverend Zeisberger was taken to the Wyandot War Chief Kuhn, from Lower Sandusky, while Reverend Senseman was taken to the War Chief Snip, from Upper Sandusky. Hopocan took Reverend Heckewelder. Each missionary was placed, naked, under a hastily erected bark lean-to just as it started to rain. Women brought each of the missionaries blankets and food when it got dark.

War dances went on all night all around the missionaries' make-shift shelters. The converts took advantage of the warriors' preoccupation. In the dark, they buried their farm equipment as well as saws, axes, and kitchen utensils.

The next morning, Wyandot warriors proceeded en masse to the nearby Moravian town of Salem. One of their chiefs told the Moravians, *"Your teachers are all prisoners. In a short time, my warriors will rob your property. Submit to my protection and deliver me your valuables, and I will not let anyone harm you or touch your property."* The warriors with the chief loudly yelled out their scalp yell. It was heard back in Gnadenhutten.

The Salem residents complied, but they complained to Hopocan, a chief of their own tribe, that their teachers were being mistreated. Hopocan ordered that the missionaries' black suits be given back to them, but by then, the clothes had been cut up and altered to suit the wearer. Sleeves had been cut off jackets, and legs of trousers had been shortened. Heckewelder got his coat back, but the sleeves had been shortened by a foot.

Matthew Elliot, always the trader, offered a flip penny for every pair of shoes brought to him. Goose and Black Snake raced each other around both villages collecting all boots, shoes, and moccasins, betting on who could collect the most.

Meanwhile, Matthew Elliot agreed that if the missionaries promised not to run off, he would free them. The missionaries gave their assurances that they would not, that they would remain with their flock.

Dunquat put Hopocan in charge of getting the large congregation of coverts ready to depart for Fort Detroit. The Lenape warriors rounded them up, with instructions to carry only what they needed for the long journey on foot. Dunquat also directed a hundred warriors, Wyandot and Shawnee, to search the woods to look for any buried articles. They found much of what the Moravians had buried.

The warriors tore down all the fences to let the horses graze in the nearly ripe cornfields. Pigs and chickens were slaughtered and left to rot. The corn storage was burned, using the hymnals and Bibles as fire starters. The Moravians' food supply of potatoes, cabbages, and turnips was also thrown into the fire. A whiskey cache was found. Hopocan, who had a weakness for hard liquor, thought, like many of them, that it gave him special powers, and took it upon himself to safeguard it.

Twenty canoes were loaded with plunder. Much had to be left behind. Hopocan set out on foot leading the coverts towards the remains of Coshocton.

Dunquat ordered a war party to break away and strike the settlements along the Ohio River. Knotche, Standing Tree, Black Snake, and Goose all volunteered, along with two of Dunquat's sons.

Elliot accompanied the Shawnee warriors as they headed south into Shawnee country. He planned to meet up with Hopocan and Dunquat at Fort Detroit after visiting his Shawnee wife.

The missionaries knelt and prayed and offered thanks when Elliot rode off.

23 BRANT

Joseph Brant, the Mohawk who had been leading the Iroquois against Washington's army in the east, had gotten into a drunken brawl with a British officer. Since the war had shifted to the South, Brant, commissioned as a British Officer, was transferred to the west at Fort Detroit. Even though the western tribes distrusted the Iroquois, Lt Governor DePeyster knew of Brant's reputation as an effective leader in war. He had received intelligence in which Brant, who spoke good English, could be useful: the feared Kentuckian George Rogers Clark, recently promoted to Brigadier General of the Virginia militia, was raising an army to attack Fort Detroit.

Brant led ninety Iroquois, Wyandot, and Shawnee warriors south to cut off Clark. They picked up more warriors on the way, including Knotche and his three friends.

&

Colonel Brodhead finally lost the battle with General Clark over who should get the limited men and resources on the frontier.

Thomas Jefferson, then Governor of Virginia, had told Washington that he doubted that Clark and Brodhead should combine forces. He had faith in the capabilities of Clark, but he didn't know Brodhead. He suggested to Washington that if he thought Brodhead was more likely to be successful against the British at Fort Detroit, then, by all means, send him and divert Clark somewhere else useful.

Washington deferred to Jefferson. He ordered Brodhead to provide his artillerymen and any supplies he had to spare to General Clark, if requested. Washington pointed out that Clark was not an officer of the Continental line, but that his reputation was "justly acquired" and that the "instructions he received are calculated to promote the general good."

At the beginning of March, General Clark arrived at Fort Pitt and began recruiting men for an expedition against the British. He set up his headquarters in the home of Washington's old friend, Colonel William Crawford. Clark immediately ran into problems. The officials in Pennsylvania didn't like a Virginian from the far western county of Kentucky coming to their area to recruit Pennsylvania men. A riot erupted. The militia of three Virginia counties refused to provide men. Both the Pennsylvanians and the Virginians were worried that if the men left on an expedition, their families would be vulnerable to Indian attack from the north and west, or from Lord Cornwallis to the east and south.

One county near Fort Pitt agreed to provide three-hundred men commanded by Colonel Archibald Lochry. Many in the area believed that the only way to stop the Indian attacks was to capture Fort Detroit. But Lochry could only sign up eighty-three volunteers.

Instead of waiting for Lochry to recruit more men and anxious to begin the campaign as soon as possible, General Clark headed downriver from Fort Pitt with the men he had. He expected Colonel Lochry to catch up with him in a few days. Clark planned to stop at Fort Henry to recruit more militiamen and obtain supplies. His goal had been to raise an army of two-thousand men. None of the Wetzels were enticed to join Clark. They didn't know him. Clark waited for Lochry longer than he had anticipated but had to leave Fort Henry when his men started deserting. Lochry arrived at Fort Henry the day after Clark and his soldiers had gone downriver.

Lochry sent a note on ahead by canoe that he was short on supplies. Clark sent a note back that he would proceed slowly so Lochry could catch up.

More men deserted Clark, and they fled back upriver, right into Lochry's flatboats. Lochry took sixteen of them prisoner.

At the mouth of the Kanawha River, Clark stopped briefly but found he had to keep moving when more men deserted. He left a note for Lochry.

Lochry sent one of his officers, Captain Shannon, and seven men on ahead in canoes with a note asking Clark to leave him more food. He was running short, and he didn't want to waste any time by sending out hunters. The next day, though, with Shannon not back and the men grumbling about lack of food, he sent out two hunters. They never returned.

Brant and his warriors hid along the north bank of the Great Miami River as his Shawnee scouts reported Clark and his large force of over four-hundred soldiers coming downriver. Brant didn't have enough warriors for a successful attack. Goose volunteered to deliver a message to the British Superintendent of Indian Affairs at Fort Detroit, Alexander McKee, for reinforcements. Goose rode as fast as he could and passed along the message without problems. He continued on to his village to see Danelle. She was pregnant and would have nothing to do with him. He returned to Fort Detroit in time to join the reinforcements.

McKee hurriedly organized a party and appointed Simon Girty's brother George, to lead it. Along with his three brothers, Simon Girty had been captured by the Seneca when they were children. The Girty boys had been doled out to various tribes. George had been raised by the Lenape.

Before the reinforcements could get there, Clark and his men, on flatboats, passed by Brant and his warriors waiting in ambush. Most of the warriors were asleep, and the two assigned to watch the river for any Long Knives didn't see them. It was pitch black dark, no moon, and Clark's men were sleeping, too, except those on watch and steering.

The next morning, Black Snake spotted the two canoes of Captain Shannon and his seven men. The Shawnee warriors in Brant's party were experts at river warfare. Under Standing Tree's direction, the warriors hid while Brant and George Girty put on hats to hide their hair and stood on the shore in a cleared, open area. They were dressed like Englishmen. Brant called out in the King's English, "Ahoy there, friends. I am in need of assistance."

"Gawd, are we glad as heck to see you," Girty called out.

The two canoes angled into shore, where they were captured at gunpoint. Knotche found a note on Captain Shannon addressed to General Clark. Brant read it and learned that Lochry was not far behind.

No sooner were those men taken prisoner than another group of six men led by Major Cracraft, from Lochry's detachment, were captured in the same fashion.

Brant decided to set a trap for Lochry, following Standing Tree's advice once again, only this time they forced the new captives to stand in plain sight at the river's edge.

Lochry's flatboats hadn't stopped in two days. His men were hungry, and his horses needed to be fed. He sent out hunters, and they killed a buffalo. He assigned other men to cut fresh grass for the horses. One thing he didn't do was assign guards to stand watch. Nobody saw Standing Tree's trap and the captives standing on the shore. They floated right on by.

Black Snake turned to Knotche. *"Are they blind?"*

"There is no telling with Long Knives," Knotche replied. *"Their minds are weak."*

"They don't pay attention," stated Standing Tree.

"I would have bet money that we would have them all," Black Snake said.

"You would have lost," added Knotche.

Brant immediately shifted strategy. He and his warriors raced ahead with plans to sneak up on Lochry's men if they landed towards dark. They followed the flatboats, staying out of sight. Lochry's company pulled ashore at dusk to set up camp. When

Brant had the warriors in position, he called on them to open fire. The Americans were taken by complete surprise. Some didn't have their muskets handy. Some fought back until their ammunition ran out. Others tried to flee by river, but Standing Tree had warned of that possibility and canoes full of warriors were ready to intercept them.

Colonel Lochry, seeing that there no way to escape, called on his men to surrender. Thirty-seven were killed. Sixty-four were taken prisoner. Lochry was sitting on a log in shock when a Wyandot warrior walked up behind him and whacked him in the head with his tomahawk. Standing Tree knocked the tomahawk from the warrior's hand, but it was too late. Lochry was dead.

"This battle is over," Standing Tree said, addressing the others. *"These men are our prisoners. We kill fighting men. Not men who have surrendered."* He glowered around at all of them.

Brant agreed with Standing Tree and ordered that there would be no more killing. All the dead were scalped, and the bodies were left for the vultures and wolves.

The prisoners, with hands tied, were marched upriver. They headed north, still in pursuit of General Clark. They met up with three-hundred warriors led by McKee and one-hundred British rangers. A few warriors were left to guard the prisoners. The rest, including Knotche, Black Snake, Goose, and Standing Tree, took off in pursuit of Clark.

Nearly two weeks later, Brant's force was still trying to catch Clark when Black Snake spotted two white men. He and Knotche hid behind two trees, and when the men walked by, they captured them at gunpoint. They brought them to Brant and McKee. The prisoners were interrogated. They told Brant that General Clark had called off the expedition because of a shortage of men.

24 YELLOW CREEK

The warriors were a long way from home, anybody's home. They traveled together along the Wabash trail, on the lookout for trouble. They set up camp on a hill overlooking the Ohio River, where a large peach grove grew.

Goose was on his fourth peach, with juice dripping down his chin. *"This is the best fruit. I love these. What are they called?"*

Black Snake shrugged. He, too, was eating one after the other.

Knotche said, *"We call them peachsanck. These are nice and juicy. I've never had them ripe off the tree before.*

"I'm bringing some seeds with me. My mother would love them," Goose said, his mouth full and juice dripping down his chin onto his belly.

"Don't make yourself sick," Black Snake said. *"Whose fruit grove is this?"*

Standing Tree said, *"These were planted by the Shawnee. The Miami and the Shawnee take care of all this land. All along the Wabash up to their villages at Auglaize, Little Turtle is the chief."* He reached up and picked a ripe fruit. He took a bite and closed his eyes. *"Mmmm!"*

By morning, Standing Tree was the only one not running off into the woods every few minutes to relieve themselves. He had only eaten one the day before and another one in the morning.

161

The band continued up a narrow valley. They mounted a hill and stopped to rest before crossing the Miami River. From there, they took the trail that led to the Shawnee towns. Standing Tree and several other of the Shawnee left the band to head to their homes on the Scioto.

Knotche, Black Snake, and Goose continued on the trail headed northeast towards Coshocton. The weather was pleasant, and they walked along in small groups or pairs, talking. The three friends discussed going up to Pluggy's Town, but none of them could find a reason to go there.

"I'm not stopping," said Knotche. *"Corn Tassel is expecting me to come home and provide for her and the baby."*

"You're calling my village your home now?" Goose asked.

"I have no other home," Knotche replied. *"Your sister is my wife. I have no other family. It wouldn't be safe to bring her to Kuskuskee. It's too close to the Long Knife devils."*

"I'm not going back there. Not for a while. Danelle won't have me, and it breaks my heart every time I see her."

Black Snake shrugged. *"I haven't been home in a long time. Come home with me. I'll introduce you to my cousins. Maybe one of them will fill the hole in your heart."*

Goose didn't answer. They walked along silently. After several minutes, Black Snake said, *"Whatever happened with the story you were telling us about the ganyo gowa? Was that the end?"*

Knotche replied. *"Those are winter stories. We tell them when we need entertainment. I'll tell you the rest another time. But I'll tell you this much - there's more. Now, we have this delightful day and each other's company to entertain us. We don't need stories."*

It was a safe, pleasant walk after a hard journey chasing the Long Knives. Occasionally, they came upon a Mingo, Lenape, or Shawnee village and stopped to hear the latest news, so they weren't surprised that there was nothing but ashes left of Coshocton when they arrived.

When they reached the fork in the trail, Knotche said, *"I will see you again, my noble brothers,"* and took the fork in the trail heading north. Black Snake and Goose continued, knowing that there was no point in stopping at Gnadenhutten for a good meal and shelter. Those days were over.

They continued towards Yellow Creek.

"I was surprised when you told me you were related to James Logan. Why did those white devils do that?"

Black Snake shrugged. *"Who knows why they do what they do? Don't tell anyone this. This is a secret between you and me. Deal? You have to promise. I've never told anyone this. Promise me?"*

"Of course," Goose said. *"You have my word."*

"Some friends and I," Black Snake said, *"saw these white men cross the Ohio River on horses one evening. At Yellow Creek, where we're heading. We were out frog hunting. We were just kids, you know, out having a good time. We knew they had no business being on our side of the river. We should have told somebody, and maybe things would have turned out differently. I wish we had. Who knows how things would have turned out?"*

"We just go where the Spirit directs us," Goose replied.

"Yes, that's true. What happened wasn't my idea. I just went along. We thought that this was a good chance to get a horse. There were three of them, three white men all on horses. One for each of us.

We waited until they were asleep. It was Hawkeye's idea, so he went first. He was thirteen-winters-old. He crawled up to their camp where they had their horses hobbled and untied one and was leading it away when it reared up. We didn't know, but there were bells tied to the horses, and the bell clanged loudly and woke the Long Knives up. They fired their rifles at Hawkeye. Killed him.

"My other buddy, Clatchy, and I started running. One of the men in our village heard the gunshots and came running to see what was going on. He didn't know there were white men there. I wish we had stopped him and told him, but we were scared. He ran right into their camp, and they shot him, too.

"Those three white devils broke camp and galloped out of there and swam their horses across. Didn't even bother with the crossing, they were in such a hurry. Just galloped right into the river and swam their horses to the other side.

"Next morning, I didn't know what to do. I couldn't sleep that night. I lay awake thinking about Hawkeye. He was my friend. My best friend. I heard lots of gun firing, and I jumped out of bed. It was coming from across the river, at Baker's Trading Post. We used to go over there to buy supplies. A bunch of men got in two canoes and went over to investigate what was going on because Logan's family had gone over earlier to buy supplies. *Two of them were killed before they knew what was happening, and another group tried to paddle over there, but there were too many Long Knives firing their muskets, and they had to turn back. Logan lost his family. His wife, brother, sister, nephew. Everyone."*

"That's terrible. Logan had the right to seek revenge," Goose said.

"Yes, he did. But I've felt guilty about it ever since. If I had told somebody, we might have avoided a war."

"How old were you?"

"It was my twelfth year."

Goose put his arm on Black Snake's shoulder. "That's a heavy burden."

They walked along in silence for the rest of the day. Once they passed the vacant town of Gnadenhutten, there were no more villages. None of the tribes wanted to live near the river because it flooded so often. Also, they didn't want to be too close to the Long Knives.

It had been years since Black Snake had been home. There was no one there, no one had been living there in a long time. The wigwams were falling down and overgrown, with trees growing right out of them.

"Well, that's just great!" Exclaimed Goose. *"You're going to introduce me to your cousins! What? Are they snakes? Bugs? I should have known! I walk for weeks with you, and what do I get? Nothing!"* The long trip and disappointments came cascading out of him. He pushed Black Snake's shoulder, harder than he'd meant to.

"Hey! It's not my fault?"

"If it's not your fault, whose fault is it?" Goose shoved him again.

"Hey, watch it!"

"Oh, yeah? What are you going to do about it?" Goose shoved him again.

Black Snake grabbed Goose's hand and bent it back at the wrist, forcing Goose to his knees.

"Ow!" Goose grabbed Black Snake's leg with his free hand, sending Black Snake tumbling. They wrestled each other, hitting and kicking, and neither could get the advantage over the other. They fought until they had nothing left to fight with, but neither gave up.

25 ESCAPE

Martin Wetzel, Lewis' oldest brother, had learned much of the language and customs of the Shawnee. After his capture, he had been adopted into the tribe and was considered by them as one of their own. He was given most of the rights and privileges of a member of the tribe. As time went on, he gained more and more of their trust.

One day, soon after his return home from chasing General Clark and leaving Knotche and his friends, Standing Tree and two other warriors made plans to go on a hunt. They needed meat for the winter.

"Come with us, brother," Standing Tree said to Martin. Standing Tree thought highly of the white man. Martin had adopted the ways of the Shawnee and proven himself to be capable. Everyone had told him that Wetzel had been helpful and courteous in his absence, and they had grown to like him. *"Let us see what kind of hunter you are. Perhaps we can teach each other something new."*

Although he was free to come and go as he pleased, Martin still felt like he was a prisoner. He wasn't allowed to go anywhere alone. Going on this hunt was no exception. He was always looking for a way to escape, but no opportunity had presented itself. But he hadn't given up trying. He was lonely for the company of his friends and family and didn't consider himself a Shawnee at all.

The four headed south and set up a hunting camp in a place the Shawnee knew. It had good spring water, willows to stretch skins, and plenty of firewood. Each day, the hunters set off alone and returned in the evening with whatever catch they had managed to find. The plan was to cache a good supply of meat, then cross the river to the Kentuck land to steal horses from the trespassers to carry the meat back home.

Martin could see that this might present the opportunity he was looking for. What held him back was that he knew that these Shawnee were superb hunters and trackers and that they knew this land, and he was still learning it. He doubted he could make it back to Wheeling before they caught him. And he knew from the stories he'd heard all his life that if they captured him a second time, it wouldn't be pretty. He remembered what they had done to John Wolf. But he couldn't stop thinking about escaping, and he finally came up with a plan.

One day, on his way back carrying the meat of an elk, he came across Standing Tree, who was loaded down with the meat of a bear. They stopped to rest and chat.

Standing Tree looked over Wetzel's catch. The meat was wrapped up in the elk skin. He pointed to the bullet hole. *"That's a nice shot."*

"My father taught me since I was a boy how to shoot. I don't waste bullets. He always stressed reloading quickly, too."

"I would like to see that," said Standing Tree, having grown to trust Martin. It wasn't in his constitution to consider trickery. It never crossed his mind. What a person said was to be believed, and he considered

Martin a Shawnee, somebody whose word was true and in whose hands he could put his life.

Martin loaded up his gun. *"See that branch?"* Martin pointed to the tip of an oak branch high up in the tree.

Standing Tree nodded. *"That's not an easy shot."* The leaves shook as the bullet hit the branch, cutting off the leaves at the tip. Before the leaves hit the ground, Martin reloaded and fired again, cutting off another stem of leaves farther down the branch.

Standing Tree smiled widely as Martin loaded again. *"I'm impressed. That's an amazing feat!"*

Martin suddenly swung the rifle barrel at Standing Tree's chest and pulled the trigger. Standing Tree had no time to react. It happened so fast. He was thrown backwards by the jolt of the bullet. His eyes opened wide before he collapsed on the ground on his back.

Martin walked over and kicked him. To make sure he was dead, he slit his throat before pulling the body and Standing Tree's bear meat under a bush and piled leaves and sticks on it. Then, he gathered up his elk meat and hurried on to camp.

He was the first one back. He gathered firewood, set some elk on spits, and began cooking some and slicing some thin and drying it. When the other two returned before dark, each with venison, Martin asked, *"Where's Standing Tree?"*

Fish Hawk and Grey Wolf both laughed.

"Who knows? Standing Tree can take care of himself," Grey Wolf said. *"Knowing him, he probably went after a bear."*

Fish Hawk agreed. *"No need to worry about him, little brother. Let's eat."*

The next day, when the two Shawnee went out again to hunt, Martin followed Grey Wolf. Pretending that he had just accidentally come across him, he walked up to him.

"Did you see that deer?" Martin asked casually.

"Where?"

Martin pointed to the east at the same time he pulled out his tomahawk and swung it down on top of Grey Wolf's head. He slit Grey Wolf's throat. He pulled the body next to a log and covered it with leaves, and returned to camp.

When Fish Hawk came trudging into camp under a load of wood-buffalo meat, Martin ran over to him. *"Here! Let me help you."*

As Fish Hawk bent down to drop some of the heavy load on the ground, Martin whipped out his tomahawk and whacked Fish Hawk in the head. He slit his throat, too, and dragged him away from camp and covered him with leaves.

That night, Martin leisurely ate buffalo steaks. The next morning, he set out for the river. He crossed the river and went to the nearest settlement.

The people there thought he was an Indian. He looked like an Indian. He dressed like an Indian, and they were all for shooting him.

"Wait. I'm a white man, I'm telling you. I'm a friend of Boone's. Call him. He'll vouch for me."

Half the men wanted to kill him on the spot, but he did speak good English, so the other half agreed to his request, and Daniel Boone was sent for.

Boone showed up, and after a quick conversation, declared, "I know this man. This is Martin Wetzel, from

Wheeling. We've been on expeditions together." They released Martin, and he returned upriver to Wheeling.

26 EXPEDITION

While the Moravians were being moved to British territory, the war in the east had taken an unexpected turn. British general Lord Cornwallis, five-hundred miles southeast of Gnadenhutten, found himself trapped at Yorktown.

The French Navy prevented British ships from coming to Lord Cornwallis' rescue. American and French troops, led by General Washington, bombarded the British troops for several days before Cornwallis was forced to surrender the British army.

The tribes in the Ohio country, when they heard that news, were thrown into total confusion. Did they again align with the wrong power as they'd done in the French and Indian War when they sided with the French? In councils throughout the Ohio country, they all came to the same conclusion. They had no choice but to continue to fight for their cause, their lifestyle, and their land even without British help. They hadn't surrendered, and the cause they were fighting for, protecting their land from invaders, was as valid as ever. Raids on the border settlements continued through the fall and into the winter. The British continued to supply them.

The belief among the frontier people living from Fort Pitt to Fort Henry was that when the trouble wasn't from the Seneca up the Allegheny River, it was from the Indians living closest to them. And since most of the traditional Lenape had been wiped out by Brodhead or had fled up north, it had to be the Moravian converts. The general feeling, all along the frontier, was that no Indian could be trusted. And even if the Moravians weren't directly involved, it was generally known that they helped out the war parties. That was true. The Moravians tried to follow the stories of Jesus as they understood Him from the teachings of the missionaries. They had provided food and water to anyone who passed through their village, whether peaceful or not, and often bought plundered goods. The spoils of war had been the only goods available to them until the Lenape aligned with the British since the Americans never had anything to trade.

Unaware that the Lenape Moravian converts had been evacuated by Half King Dunquat and Hopocan, Lt. Colonel David Williamson organized an expedition to break up the Moravian villages. Lewis signed up, hoping for a chance to take a few scalps without much risk, and get paid to do it.

Eighty volunteers crossed over the river at Mingo Bottoms, and by the next day, they were at the Tuscarawa River only to find the Moravian towns almost entirely deserted. There were a few people still there who hadn't left with Hopocan, people who had been out hunting or visiting relatives and had missed the evacuation. Williamson and his men rounded up all they could find and took them to Fort Pitt as prisoners.

Lt. Col. Williamson personally rode behind the prisoners to keep an eye on them. He wouldn't allow a vote on what to do with the captives, knowing what his men would do to these Indians, Christian or not. Lewis Wetzel, and many others, wanted to kill the prisoners anyway but never had the opportunity. They came back without any scalps.

Upon their return, the frontier people ridiculed Williamson and his men for being too lenient. To make matters worse, the prisoners were treated well by the new Commandant of the Western District, Colonel John Gibson.

Gibson had taken over command of the Western District at Fort Pitt in May after General Washington had removed Brodhead for his misuse of funds and subsequent court-martial. Gibson, who had befriended Chief White Eyes and found his body, later commanded Fort Laurens and stopped the starving soldiers from mutiny. He was sympathetic to all indigenous people and the Lenape in particular, having personally known and lived with them when he was captured during Pontiac's Rebellion and adopted by the Lenape.

The new Commandant apologized to the Moravians for taking them away from their homes. He fed them, clothed them, and thanked them for being supporters of the American cause. He directed the Continental soldiers to escort them back to their homes.

27 PROMISE

British authorities sought to keep pressure on the Americans. The majority of the Moravians had been moved to British territory, thereby eliminating the missionary spies' influence. Not realizing yet that Cornwallis' defeat signaled the end of the war, DePeyster sent Hopocan out on a raiding party into western Pennsylvania. They knew the Americans wouldn't be expecting an attack this late in the fall, and now there were no spies to warn them. Hopocan sought to use that surprise to the British advantage. Knotche declined to go. He was a father now and felt his duty was to stay home with his wife and baby daughter.

After the fight with Black Snake, Goose crossed the river alone, intent on finding a horse to ride back home on. He was tired of walking. He built himself a canoe and paddled across in the dark and found five horses right across the river near Baker's Trading post. They were in a barn locked up for the night because the weather had turned cold. He walked into the barn, found a bag of corn, and made friends with the horses with it. He hadn't intended to take all of them, just the black stallion he liked, but he left their stables and the barn door open just to cause havoc when he quietly walked away. The other horses followed him. Once he crossed the river, he kept on going, remembering what had happened the last time, when the river proved to no longer provide protection.

Black Snake had nowhere to go. He had no home. He was feeling blue after his fight with Goose. Goose had been his friend. He couldn't figure out what had happened. It wasn't his fault that his people were gone from Yellow Creek. It had been a long time since he had been home. Where were they? He was lonely. The sudden cold snap reminded him that it would soon be a good time to hunt because the winter furs paid well, but what did that matter? There was no reason to go to that trouble, nobody to buy presents for and nothing he needed. So he wandered towards Pluggy's Town just to be around other people. Maybe someone there would know where his family was. Once there, he built himself a wigwam and settled in for the winter, occasionally going out to hunt for food. After a meager existence for several months, not finding anything worth living for, he decided to go visit Knotche at the Lakes. Maybe his luck would change. He knew the hunting would be good on the way, and he could pick up some furs to buy more lead and powder for his new musket. He couldn't think of a reason not to go, so he went.

Hopocan's warriors took scalps and burned cabins in the scattered settlements across the Ohio River and then headed back across the river into safe territory. To confuse any pursuers, instead of going straight back to the Sandusky towns where Hopocan and his warriors now lived with Dunquat and the Wyandot, they fled into familiar territory. The few Moravians that Colonel Gibson had escorted home had all gone to Shoenbruen, a Moravian village in the same general area as the others. Hopocan and his band stopped at the abandoned town of Ghadenhutten to water their horses.

The Moravians who had been evacuated by Dunquat and Hopocan weren't doing well in the land of plenty that Dunquat had promised. It didn't turn out to be a land of abundance. Their cornucopia was back at Ghadenhutten and the other Moravian villages. They ran short of food. Prices of food had skyrocketed now that the French and the British battled for control of the seas. The Moravians begged to be allowed to return to their villages to harvest their corn crop. It had never been harvested. Surely there was corn still left standing in the fields. They were starving. They needed it. Dunquat granted their request if they promised to return.

Over a hundred Moravians went south to harvest any corn still edible from the fields at Ghadenhutten, Salem, and Shoenbruen. They had left the fields full of corn. They hoped and prayed there would still be some left.

Black Snake had made himself some snowshoes and was making good time. He was getting some practice with his British musket and hadn't gone hungry yet,

177

although it was noisy, and he wondered if he had enough lead and powder to get him to the Lakes. The more he thought about it, the more he didn't really want to fool with furs. He didn't want to carry them. He didn't need to buy anybody gifts. All he needed was a little lead and powder. That wouldn't cost much. He knew he could rely on Goose's trick of trapping raccoons, so at least he wouldn't starve.

He was cursing his bad luck as he traipsed along, wishing he had some company. He was lonely. He didn't care to spend his life by himself. His idea of adventure included other people. He was wondering how he'd ended up like this when he suddenly came upon the large band of Moravians walking towards him, leading a herd of horses.

They weren't going in the same direction, but he didn't really care, so he turned around and walked with them, thanking the spirit for this fluke, this happy change of events.

Isaac approached him. *"You are Mingo."*

"Yes, Grandfather."

"I have seen you with a young friend of mine. He goes by the name Knotche."

"Yes, Grandfather. He is a good friend. We are like brothers."

Black Snake explained that Knotche had married and his wife was expecting a baby, so he had gone to the Lakes. He was hoping to see him soon and had been headed that way.

"Then you should come with us. We will be returning that way soon. Perhaps you would like to join us. We are the way of peace. We believe that the living God, Jesus Christ, will show you the way. Come with us, my son."

Others joined the two. A woman reached out and took his hand. It was warm. He looked at her. She was an attractive, young woman.

Instead of finding the warmth of human companionship he wanted, though, Black Snake distrusted these people. He liked the traditional ways. He wasn't even sure he liked using a modern musket instead of the traditional bow and arrows. The musket was so noisy, and it smelled, and it scared the animals. He had always thought the Moravians were a bit crazy for giving up their traditional ways and becoming like the whites. It made more sense to him that there was spirit in everything. That belief had made him humble and grateful, yet proud of who he was.

When the woman whispered to him, *"Won't you take Jesus into your heart?"* And she squeezed his hand, he pulled his hand away like he'd been burned.

"This is the way I'm going," he said. He pointed off into the snow-covered forest.

"Good-bye, then, young friend," said Isaac.

Several of them called to him. *"Peace be with you!"*

"Jesus loves you!"

"May the Lord bless you!"

He hurried into the woods as fast as he could on his snowshoes, cursing his bad luck.

28 GOOSE'S RETURN

Goose's trip north with the horses had been a miserable trip in the cold, but he had been luckier than he knew. There had been no new snow, and the weather had stayed cold, keeping the ground hard. He stopped at the deserted Moravian village of Salem when he noticed corn still standing in the fields. He rode his horses into an empty barn and then went out and picked corn to feed to them. Once they were taken care of, he made himself at home in an empty cabin. It was so comfortable he ended up sticking around for a couple of days. He had a bed and dry wood for the fire and plenty of food for the horses.

If it hadn't been for wanting to see Danelle, he might have stayed longer. But now that he had what he was sure was a suitable dowry, he was anxious to get home.

He whooped loudly as he got close to his village. Goose had never been so proud. He came trotting up to the council house atop the black stallion leading the four horses. Everyone came out of their cabins to see the noise. He waved to Knotche and Corn Tassel and his mother, and when he spotted Danelle, he sat up even straighter. She would now be his. He was sure of it. What good fortune had come his way! If five horses wasn't a fitting enough dowry, nothing was.

After eating a good, hot meal of fish at his mother's cabin, with Knotche and Corn Tassel and their baby, he went to Danelle's cabin just as it was getting dark.

He called out to her, *"Danelle! It's me. Goose. Can I come in?"*

"Yes, but don't let the cold in."

He ducked quickly through the fur skin, covering the doorway. There was a fire going, and it was warm, but it was too dark to see well.

"It's so good to see you!" He held out his arms wide, but she ignored him. *"Aren't you happy to see me?"* He pouted.

"Hey, Goose." The trader, Pierre Peltier, had been laying down on the bench next to the wall. He sat up. *"You've done well for yourself. I saw you ride in."*

Goose was shocked. He looked at the trader, then at Danelle, then back at the trader. *"What are you doing here?"*

"No, Goose," Pierre replied. *"The question is, what are you doing here."*

Thinking fast, Goose said, *"I've just come to say hello to my old friend Danelle. I haven't seen her in a while."*

"You know she's my wife?"

"Yes. Of course I know that. Congratulations!"

Danelle served both men tea. Goose politely made small talk as he tried to figure out what to do. She'd told him she'd gotten married, but he didn't really believe it and definitely didn't think he'd still be around. Danelle was his, not some white man's. And now he'd brought her what she wanted, a dowry worthy of her. Why couldn't she just tell him to leave? He wasn't even Wyandot. Finally, when enough time had passed to be polite, he said his goodbyes, feeling dejected, and returned to his mother's cabin.

29 CAPTURE

L t. Colonel Williamson, still smarting from the ridicule he had received in the spring campaign into the Moravian towns, called for volunteers to pursue Hopocan and his raiders. One hundred and sixty militiamen signed up. Uncle Lewis Bonnett joined. One of the Greathouse brothers volunteered. Martin Wetzel agreed to go. Lewis refused. Joining the army and killing Indians didn't seem to go together from his latest experience. To Lewis' way of thinking, Williamson just didn't get it about Indians. And if Lewis did kill an Indian, the army wanted to arrest him. He would do it his own way.

The Western District Commander, Colonel Gibson, sent a messenger to Shoenbruen. He told the Moravians whom he'd had escorted back to their village to be on the alert. The militia were coming. By then, unknown to Gibson, a hundred more Moravians led by Isaac had returned. They dismissed the warning. They had done nothing wrong. God would protect them. But they armed themselves, at Isaac's suggestion, just in case. The Moravians had divided up and were gathering the corn at their three settlements in Gnadenhutten, Salem, and Schoebrun when the militia arrived.

The militiamen, with expert trackers like Lewis Bonnett and Martin Wetzel along, had followed Hopocan's war party tracks to Gnadenhutten. Hopocan and his raiding party had already come and gone before the large group of Moravians had arrived. The tracks leading to the Moravian village reconfirmed Williamson's belief that the Moravians were guilty of the recent attack. Williamson made camp a mile away from Gnadenhutten and drew up a quick plan while scouts were sent out to reconnoiter.

Half the troops would divide into three smaller groups and attack the village from three directions. The other half would cross over the Tuscarawas River and attack the Indians working in the cornfields. No one would be allowed to escape.

The men crossing the river ran into unexpected obstacles. The river was too high to wade across, and it was filled with floating ice. They spotted what looked like a canoe on the opposite shore. One young man volunteered to swim across and fetch it. It turned out to be, not a canoe, but a large sap trough used to collect maple syrup in the spring. But it floated, and they were able to plug up both ends and cross the river in it, two men at a time. Others swam across, while those in the make-shift canoe kept the muskets and powder dry for the swimmers.

Sixteen of them had crossed when they spotted a Lenape teenager. Three men shot at him. One bullet hit him, breaking the boy's arm. At the sound of gunfire, the rest of the militiamen scrambled across the river, and word was sent to those approaching the town to attack without delay, fearing that the shots would alert the Moravians.

The wounded boy, Joseph, looked up at the militiamen with frightened eyes. He pleaded in English. "I am the son of a white man. Please!" He held his hands up in prayer.

Three tomahawks came down on him. They chopped him to pieces and scalped him. The sixteen militiamen then ran into the field, expecting their buddies to be right behind them.

Another Moravian who was busy tying a bundle of corn stalks saw them coming and started to hail them when he saw one of the militiamen fire his musket at another Moravian. He took off, running, and hid in the bushes.

As the militiamen came closer to the workers in the field, they saw that they were vastly outnumbered. Lt. Colonel Williamson, thinking fast on his feet, whispered, "Anybody speak these buggers' language?"

Martin Wetzel nodded. "I do, sir."

Williamson told him what to say. Martin told the others to smile friendly-like.

Martin held up his hand in greeting and addressed them in a welcoming manner.

"Good day, my Christian brothers!" He said, speaking in Algonquin. *"We have come to take you to Fort Pitt. It is very dangerous here today."*

The Moravian farmers gathered around the militiamen.

"We have come to take you to safety," continued Martin. *"We love you."*

One woman said, *"This is the hand of God. The Americans have come to rescue us."*

An older man said, *"Praise the Lord that there are such true friends as yourselves."*

Other Moravians chimed in with heartfelt thanks.

The other half of the militiamen entered the village. They found it nearly empty. One woman ran and hid in the bushes. They chased her down and shot her. They took one man captive. Everyone else was working in the fields or had gone to one of the other Moravian towns.

The militiamen escorted the villagers who had been working in the fields through town, past the church. Williamson requested that they turn over their weapons, and they would be returned to them once they reached the safety of Fort Pitt. They readily did so. The militiamen helped the villagers pack up their valuables, including their communion wine, for the journey to Fort Pitt. They then separated the men from the women.

One of the native leaders, John Martin, sent a messenger to Salem to tell them what was happening. He told them that a group of soldiers would come over and escort them back to Gnadenhutten. Trusting the militiamen, Salem's farmers came back with the militiamen, talking to each other about love and miracles and the answer to prayers. The Moravians at Schoebrun had been forgotten.

When they reached the riverbank, the Salem Moravians saw blood on the sand. They were immediately suspicious. The militiamen seized them and confiscated their weapons. The men were sent to one house, the women to another, where the others who had already been captured were being held captive.

The next day, the captives were all assembled in the wide street in front of the church. The militiamen surrounded them with loaded muskets at the ready lest their prisoners try to escape.

With Lt. Colonel Williamson's consent, a trial was held to decide what to do with the captives. All the Moravians were charged with stealing horses, axes, spoons, pots and pans, and everything else they possessed. They were accused of being enemy warriors, not Christians.

Isaac professed their innocence. *"These material goods are gifts from the Lord for our hard work. We are honest, God-fearing people and have harmed no one."*

Martin translated.

Williamson turned to the militiamen. "What say you?"

"Guilty," shouted nearly everyone.

Lt. Colonel Williamson, exercising his authority, asked, "Should the Indians be taken to Fort Pitt or be put to death? All in favor of taking them to Fort Pitt, step forward."

Eighteen men stepped forward. The rest remained standing where they were.

"Then, in the power vested in me," Williamson announced, "I sentence you all to death. Take them away."

Some understood English, but Martin translated anyway. There were cries and shrieks and protests.

The militiamen, pointing loaded muskets at the group, barked orders.

"Get moving, you red-skinned devils," said Lewis Bonnett.

"Move it," ordered Martin Wetzel in Algonquin.

Meanwhile, back at Fort Pitt, Colonel Brodhead attempted to reclaim his position. In the court-martial regarding his misuse of funds, it was determined that his use of the funds was justified. He wasn't punished and returned to duty. Colonel Gibson refused to relinquish the command, and Brodhead ordered Gibson arrested for usurping his authority. When General Washington heard of what was happening in the Western District, he intervened and sent a message to Fort Pitt, removing Brodhead, who was given a new assignment and later promoted to Brigadier General.

A new Commander of the Western District was soon after assigned. William Irvine had been a surgeon aboard a British man-o-war during the French and Indian War. He had supported the Revolution from the beginning and had participated in the invasion of Canada at Quebec with General Richard Montgomery and Colonel Benedict Arnold. Irvine was captured in that battle and spent nearly two years as a British prisoner of war. A month after his release, he distinguished himself at the Battle of Monmouth when the Americans attacked the British rear as they abandoned Philadelphia. Now, he was promoted to Brigadier General and assigned to take over the command of the Western District. In the east, the war was considered all but over while peace negotiations were going on in Paris.

30 MASSACRE

Hopocan heard that a teenager had arrived from Gnadenhutten. He went to talk with him, hoping to hear news of his friend Glickican, now called Isaac, and the other Moravians who had gone back to their villages for food. Hopocan was a seasoned warrior and had fought against the British, Americans, and the Iroquois. He had taken many scalps and had seen many warriors killed. He was hardened against blood and gore, but his legs felt wobbly and his head light when he saw the boy. Tears streamed down his cheeks, glistening on the blue dots of the tattoos around his mouth.

He took the boy's hand gently and sat on the ground next to him. "My *son*," he said. *"Who did this to you?"*

The dirty linen bandages covering the boy's head had been removed, and the jagged cut on top of his head was full of pus and a light-red oozing fluid. The boy looked at Hopocan. The pupils of his brown eyes were large and black. Hopocan recognized the fear and shock and squeezed his hand.

The boy tried to speak, but only sobs came out every time he opened his mouth.

"I will stay with you," Hopocan said softly. *"I will not leave your side."*

The boy slept, and when he awoke, Hopocan was still there holding his hand.

"It was the Long Knives," the boy said. His fever had subsided. *"We were gathering the corn. They came in*

peace, they said. To protect us. We gave them our weapons, and then they said we all must die."

Hopocan squeezed the boy's hand. The boy told his tale, in fits and starts.

"The old woman, Mary, knelt before their chief and begged him in the white man's tongue to spare us. That we were innocent. He told her, told all of us, 'Prepare to die.' The Long Knives called their chief William's son.

"The missionary Senseman told the white chief, 'As God is my witness, we are innocent, but we are prepared and willing to suffer death. We have all made a solemn oath at our baptism that we would only please Jesus.'

"Isaac told William's son, in the white man's language 'We ask for time to pray to him and ask for His mercy and forgiveness.'

"The white Chief granted Isaac's request.

"The men and boys were put in one house. The women and girls in another. We sang and prayed all night. We hugged each other and urged each other to be brave, to remain faithful, and that we would soon be with the Lord.

"I remember Abraham. He said to all of us, 'Dear Brothers. It seems that we shall soon meet our Savior, for our sentence is fixed. You know that I haven't always acted right and have troubled the Lord and you, too. I haven't walked the path as I should have done, but still, I will cling to my Savior with my last breath and hold Him fast even though I am a sinner. I know He will forgive me.'

"Everyone assured him of our love and forgiveness. We spent the night singing praises to God in the joyful hope that we would soon be with Him. We could hear the women singing, too.

"*In the morning, they rounded up all the men, except for the very old and very young. They tied ropes around our necks and dragged us out. Abraham was the first to go. His hair was long and tied back with a red ribbon. I heard one Long Knife say,* "That'll make a fine scalp.""

"*Moses tried to break away. He had been dancing, singing his death song while the two white men with him argued over who would get his scalp. Moses grabbed a knife from one of the whites and cut his rope, and took off running. One of the Long Knives jumped on his horse and chased Moses down. I saw Moses yank the Long Knife out of his saddle and would have killed him, too, but one of the Long Knives shot Moses and killed him.*

"*They hit me on the head with a tomahawk and scalped me, as they did to the others. I don't know why I didn't die. Do you?*" The boy sobbed softly.

Hopocan squeezed the boy's hand.

"*I lay there, thinking I must be dead. But I could see and hear everything. It must have been the Lord's will that I should live.*

"*The rest of the men were then dragged in twos and threes to what they called the killing house. It was the house where we made barrels. The big white man, Greathouse was his name, picked up the cooper's mallet and said,* 'This is the exact thing I need.'

"I couldn't see what was going on, but I heard the smacking of the mallet. After a while, I heard that Long Knife Greathouse say, 'My arm is tired. Here, go on like I have. I've done pretty well. Fourteen.'

"*When all our men and boys were killed, the Long Knives went to the house where the women were, and I heard the same thing going on. They killed us all, except those who went to Shoenbruen. Those brethren came looking for us and found me.*

Illustration from William Howell's "Stories of Ohio (1897) courtesy of the Ohio Historical Connection

"Rest, my son," Hopocan said. *"And know that another boy escaped, too, unhurt. And a few others."* Hopocan's voice turned hard and angry. He squeezed the boy's hand and stood up. *"Know that those white devils will pay for what they have done. I promise you."*

The boy smiled feebly and closed his eyes, and fell asleep.

31 THE ARMY INVADES

Word spread quickly of the successful expedition against the Indians, and nearly everyone showed up to greet the returning conquerors. Lt. Colonel Williamson and his men led sixty Moravian horses ladened down with the treasures from the Christian villages. Hurrahs were called out over and over. Not one of their champions had been harmed. Not one husband or son or father had anything more than a sore arm from swinging the cooper's mallet. There were scalps aplenty, ninety in all, though it was hard to tell a man's from a child's, not that anyone cared. Pennsylvania was offering twenty-five-hundred Continental dollars for any Indian scalps.*

None of the militiamen admitted that, out that of the ninety scalps, twenty-nine were women and thirty-nine were children. There was no doubt in anyone's mind that the scalps had once been on the heads of ruthless savages that deserved whatever they got. The treasure they had brought back had undoubtedly been stolen from white settlers and was now being returned. An auction was held, and to show support for their heroes, everyone bid liberally. The spoils were divided up, and the militia, happy with the outcome, were dismissed.

*Pennsylvania records indicate Pennsylvania only paid for a half dozen scalps during the period April 22, 1780, to March 21, 1783, when the bounty was   in   effect.

Another campaign was soon proposed to finish off the Indians with an attack on the lake towns. The new Commandant of the Western Department, General William Irvine, approved the expedition. A volunteer force was all Irvine could afford. No funds were being authorized, with the war in the east at a standstill. He had no money even for the minimal pay usually offered to the militia. Spoils would again be divided among all participants. He exempted any volunteers from two tours of militia duty. Militiamen were to provide their own horses and three days of food. Ammunition would be provided. After the successful Gnadenhutten massacre, everybody wanted to go. The volunteers met across the river from Mingo Bottoms on May 25th, and they voted on their commanding officer. The two senior officers were the militia commander Lt. Colonel Williamson and the retired Continental, Colonel William Crawford. General Irvine had asked Crawford to come out of retirement to lend his expertise.

When the militiamen voted for their Commanding Officer, Crawford received the majority of the votes. Not only was he a Continental, but he was a good friend (and real estate broker) of that foremost of Virginians, General George Washington.

The militia army, in good spirits, readied to cross the river. Martin Wetzel was anxious to go. Uncle Lewis Bonnett had volunteered, and Lewis's pals Billy Boggs and Johnny Mills also had signed up. Lewis again refused to go. He didn't care about the money. He was sick of the army, of the idea of spending more time with the army, being told to do this and do that and go here and go there and not even be able to achieve his goals. He preferred killing Indians his own way. Besides that, it was a nice summer day, a bad time to go into Indian territory.

"That's a dang nice stallion you got there, Mills," Uncle Lewis said. Like his brother-in-law John Wetzel, he was always on the lookout for good horse-flesh. "What'll you take for him?"

"Ain't for sale," Mills said. "This is one hell of a horse. Fast. Smart."

"You should breed him with one or two of my Pa's mares," Martin said. "Keep that blood-line flowing."

"I might do that," Mills replied, "if the price is right."

"He'll treat you fair, ain't that right, Uncle Lew?"

Uncle Lewis nodded.

They waded the horses across the river and led them past the remnants of wigwams of the old Mingo town and headed up the hill to the ridge-top trail. They mounted up at the top.

Black Snake had shown up just as winter was ending at the lake village with a load of raccoon furs. Knotche, and even Goose, were glad to see him. Now that he was rested and eating well, Goose's frustration and anger at Black Snake had evaporated. Black Snake was happy to be back among friends. He hadn't been there long when word reached the village that a Long Knife army was preparing to come their way. Since

Goose had horses, Hopocan gave these three trusted and experienced warriors the honor of spying on the army for him. They rode fast to the river in time to see the large group of armed men cross the river.

"Are you counting?" Goose asked Knotche.

"I can't count that high," he said, *"but I have a system."* He broke a stick and tossed a piece into a deerskin bag for every militiaman.

"Use your fingers and toes," said Black Snake. *"Instead of a stick for everyone, you could use a stick for every ten fingers and another stick for every ten toes."*

"But I only have nine fingers," Knotche declared, holding up his left hand. He proudly held up the stub of his little finger. It had been bitten off in a fight with a settler.

"Then, just count your toes," Black Snake replied.

"Or count the stub," Goose added.

"Will that work?" Knotche looked at Goose.

Goose shrugged. *"It's worth a try. You'll clean out all the kindling in the forest if you do one at a time.*

"Of course it'll work," said Black Snake. *"But I'll tell you what. You count your way, and I'll count my way, and we'll compare."*

"Why do you need a count?" Asked Goose. *"Can't we tell Hopocan there are as many Long Knives as there are stars in the sky?"*

"He wants an accurate count," said Knotche. *"He's only got a couple of handfuls of warriors. If he needs more, he wants to know how many more. But shut up. I'm losing my count."*

"He's going to need a lot more. We know that," said Goose, but the other two ignored him as they gave their attention to counting the men as they rode by.

When the last of the militiamen passed, the three warriors returned to their horses and galloped across the hilltops, circling around the trail. Knotche's and Black Snake's count differed by three. They had counted nearly five-hundred militiamen, including their officers. Goose volunteered to deliver the report. He galloped off north, while Knotche and Black Snake followed the army as it headed towards the Moravian town of Shoenbruen.

Colonel Crawford asked for volunteers to scout out ahead. He had a few scouts, like John Slover, who had been captured by the Miami when he was eight years old and had grown up among the Lenape and Shawnee, but he wasn't familiar with this country. Martin Wetzel had spent time living with the Shawnee, so he was more familiar with Indian ways than most, but he didn't know this part of the Ohio country either. Not many whites did, and no one in this army. One of the few Virginians who did was Lewis Wetzel, and he'd told Martin the army would be sitting ducks once they reached the plains.

Martin was already getting antsy riding along with the main army. He knew enough about Indians that he was sure that they were being watched. Like Lewis, he believed that you had to sneak up on Indians if you wanted to beat them, and you don't sneak up with five-hundred men in broad daylight on a hot, pleasant day. He wanted to see what was going on, not ride out in the open with a target on his back. He volunteered to be a scout.

The army camped at Shoenbruen. The fields still had last year's corn, some of it stacked and tied. They let the horses loose in the field. The horses were happy to have corn to eat. Mills kept an eye on his horse. He didn't want that stallion to eat too much and get bloated.

While they were camped, two militia captains spotted Knotche and Black Snake and shot at them. They missed, and the two took off running back to their horses. Hearing the gunshots, nearly the entire army rushed to the spot.

"I didn't know you could run this fast," Black Snake said, as the two dashed through the forest, weaving around the big trees.

"I never - had five-hundred - Long Knives - trying to - catch me," Knotche said, trying to talk, run, and breathe at the same time.

That night, Martin went to Colonel Crawford's tent. Crawford was an approachable, outgoing man, a little overweight and nearly fifty years old. He had served as an officer in the French and Indian War, served with Washington in the Virginia Rangers, served in Lord Dunmore's War, and then again as a Continental officer under Generals Hand, McIntosh, and now Irvine. He knew men well and had made it clear that any soldier could come talk to him at any time.

"Begging your pardon, Colonel."

"What is it, Private?"

"Them buggers know we're here, Colonel."

"So what? Let them. Let them come and get what we're bringing them."

"But, sir," Martin said. "That's not their way. Those buggers are watching what we do, and when they think they can get away with it, that's when they'll attack."

"Nothing I can do about that except make sure you men stay awake during your watches."

"We don't need to be walking down these Indian trails so they can set up an ambush, sir."

"I'm listening."

"Do you have a map, sir?"

Lewis had told his brother about his forays across the river and had told him about the well-traveled native trails. Martin pointed out to Colonel Crawford everything he could remember Lewis telling him about the terrain.

The next day, Colonel Crawford held a War Council with his officers to discuss a possible change in plans. He thought Wetzel had made a valid point. The officers agreed to leave the Indian trail and proceed northward, following the river, through the rocky valleys onto the plains that descended into Lake Erie.

Black Snake left Knotche to watch the Long Knives alone and galloped off to deliver this latest news that the whites were leaving the trail.

When the army descended from the rocky hills and valleys onto the plains, Crawford's scouts came across a deserted village. It was Captive Town where the Moravians evacuated by Dunquat had lived. Martin and the other scout, Slover, were both surprised. They hadn't expected to find any villages closer than Lower

Sandusky. There wasn't one on Crawford's map. Lewis hadn't mentioned to Martin anything about a town there, either. They reported their findings.

A War Council was held again. The junior officers, speaking for their men, wanted to call off the expedition. They were too deep into Indian territory, and they'd only come across a couple of Indians. They were nervous, afraid they were riding into a trap. The two senior officers, Crawford and Williamson, convinced them to keep on going a little longer, but if they didn't find any Indians by the end of the day, they would return the same way they'd come.

Goose gave his report to Hopocan, who had only a small number of warriors at his disposal. He didn't have enough to attack five-hundred soldiers. He sent out messengers to the Wyandot, the Miami, the Shawnee, the Lenape, and the Ottawa that the murderers of Gnadenhutten were invading their country, and led by the man who he presumed was the same chief, William's son. He didn't realize that, although Williamson was indeed in this invading army, he wasn't leading it. William Crawford was.

When Black Snake arrived with his report that the army had left the trail, Hopocan just said, *"Good. They won't get away now."*

Knotche soon joined them, reporting that they were not far behind him and coming forward. Hopocan sent Knotche and his two friends, and the other warriors at hand into a stand of woods on the plain where Knotche indicated that the army would pass. Hopocan told them to hide behind trees and take shots at the militiamen. It was a trick that had worked against these white armies countless times all the way back to the French and Indian War.

As the army approached the wooded area, the three friends made bets on who could shoot the most Long Knives.

"Do we need to get their scalp?" Goose asked.

Black Snake said, *"I'm not going to go out there with all those Long Knives to take a scalp. That would be suicide."*

"No," Knotche said. *"If you see your target fall, that's good enough. Agreed?*

They all nodded.

All three took careful aim. Goose shot first. Black Snake, with his new musket, then fired. Knotche's gun misfired. Only Goose hit a soldier. The other warriors also fired. Several militiamen were killed or wounded in that first barrage.

Martin and Slover were far out ahead scouting and hadn't seen the warriors hiding in the trees. At the first gunfire, they, along with others savvy in Indian warfare, including Uncle Lewis, grabbed their muskets, jumped off their horses, and ran straight towards the woods. The warriors, slow to reload, panicked and ran.

"Yow!" Cried out Goose, running like a scared rabbit.

"Wait for me," Black Snake called, but Goose didn't slow.

Knotche zig-zagged through the trees, and all three of them got away, as did most of the others. Black

Snake helped a wounded warrior shot in the leg, and they limped back to the other warriors in reserve who were watching with Hopocan.

Hopocan directed them to another stand of woods. Black Snake left the wounded man and ran towards the trees, trying to catch up with Goose and Knotche. They were spotted by Major Leet and his men, who shot at them. Knotche called for them to fall back, and they returned to Hopocan's position.

There were scattered shots fired for the rest of a very hot day, but nobody had an advantage. A few men on both sides were killed and wounded. At dark, both sides kindled fires. The militiamen followed Martin and Slover's advice to use the fires the same way the Indians did: to light up the area so attackers could be seen, but stay back away from the fires so they wouldn't be targets.

Wyandot and Lenape women began arriving with food. Knotche, Black Snake, and Goose rested and ate, and as the night progressed, they welcomed the never-ending stream of arrivals. There were Wyandot, Mingo, Lenape, Shawnee, and Ottawa arriving singly and in small and large bands.

The next morning, a few shots were fired at first light, picking off a few militiamen, but the Indian camp and the Long Knife camp were far apart and out of effective firing range. Return fire was mostly ineffective, though a few warriors were hit as well. As daylight grew, the militiamen could see bands of Indians constantly arriving. Crawford called for another War Council. No one liked the situation they found themselves in. They were far from home. The only food and ammunition they had were what they had carried.

The Indian force was growing larger by the minute. They unanimously voted to retreat.

"They'll see us retreating and attack," said Williamson. "My men aren't trained soldiers. They're liable to panic."

"We wait until dark," Crawford advised. "We bury the dead. We make litters for the wounded. We'll form in three lines, with the wounded in the middle with the main force. The scouts will lead the way. Meanwhile, have your men stay ready, but rest them. Set watches. There could be an attack at any moment."

There was no Indian attack, just random firing by both sides. But Crawford's men, looking out across the plains, could see more and more bands of Indians riding up in the distance. They were out in the open but too far away to hit with a bullet. Soon, there were Indians in front of them, on their right and their left. The only place open was behind them, the way they'd come. The militiamen were scared. Men were crying, praying, talking to themselves. Some were resting and eating and sharpening their knives and tomahawks. Others made sure their weapons worked. A few were getting drunk.

32 REVENGE

Hopocan watched and waited. He was in no hurry. He shouted out instructions to each band's leader. It was foreign to him to attack a large army with a large force of his own. To him, that was a stupid use of the valuable lives of his warriors. If he could help it, none of the warriors under his control would die unnecessarily.

Crawford ordered the dead be buried, and then fires built on top of them so that their final resting places wouldn't be found and dug up. Branches were chopped from trees to build litters to carry the wounded. Once it got dark, Crawford sent out Martin, Slover, and the other scouts to see if they could make it through behind them. They did. They rode their horses past the Indians and went for another mile before turning, picking up the Huron Trail. They left a pile of branches indicating their route, as agreed upon. They headed south on the trail. They kept riding through the deserted Moravian village of Captive Town, fairly certain that they weren't spotted.

While the scouts were exploring the way out, Colonel Crawford formed up the three lines with the wounded in the middle as planned. Some still had horses, but many horses had been lost in the first gunfire. He led the way on horseback. Lt. Colonel Williamson stayed behind with his detachment to support the line guarding the retreat. Everything proceeded smoothly. The lines were formed and moving when scattered shots rang out from the Indians' direction. No one was hit, so the militiamen guessed that it was some sort of signal. Most believed that the Indians were getting ready to attack and looked around nervously with fingers on triggers.

Those in front of the lines, leading the retreat, took off at a run, throwing up thick dust. Those right behind who followed in the dark couldn't see which way those in front had gone. They took off running, too, in a slightly different direction, not singly, but in groups of men. The majority of the army, both those carrying the casualties and the main army, walked off in an orderly but hurried manner. Behind them was Williamson's rearguard.

Those in front who had left the main army behind were the ones Hopocan had been waiting for. They ran right into his trap.

Knotche, Black Snake, and Goose, as well as warriors from several different tribes, were waiting for them.

Knotche, with his face painted yellow and black, gave out the first yell, "Aiiiii!" He whacked and chopped with his tomahawk in one hand, his knife in the other. Black Snake had a war club with wolf's teeth imbedded in the bulky, heavy end. He swung it around, clobbering soldiers left and right. Goose stood in one spot and let them come to him, whacking and chopping like Knotche with a knife in one hand, tomahawk in the other. The white men were cut to pieces in the dark among howls and screams, slicing throats and lifting scalps and tomahawks whacking at heads, chests, and arms.

Williamson's rear guard detachment fell behind and tried to catch the main army. Hopocan sent warriors to head them off, to attack them as they came. Williamson and his men broke through, with many killed or wounded, but caught up with the main army.

Colonel Crawford stayed with the main army, shouting orders when some men lagged, keeping the men together, leading them out of danger. As the night progressed, he noticed that his son John, his son-in-law William and his nephew William were no longer with him. He stopped and began asking soldiers if they had seen them. Nobody had. Crawford waited for the rear guard. Williamson and his men finally appeared, but there was still no sign of Crawford's missing relatives.

Martin, Slover, and the other advance scouts waited for the main army to catch up on the well-worn Huron Trail, but the five-hundred man army had diminished considerably, and men came running up the road like they had Beelzebub himself behind them.

"We'll ride into a trap, sure as hell, if we continue down this road," Martin announced to no one in particular. Without a word, he slapped his horse on the hindquarter, and it bolted ahead.

"Wait for me," called Slover, who didn't like the idea, either, of riding down a big, well-worn Indian trail with angry warriors somewhere out there in the dark. He took off after Martin, as did the two others.

The four militia scouts rode along in the black, starry night, going as fast as they dared. They were unable to see more than a few feet. Before they knew it, their horses were bogged down in a swamp.

Martin jumped down and sank up to his knees in warm mud.

"Dang it!" he whispered. "Don't get down."

The other three men tried to turn their horses around.

Martin pulled on the reins trying to lead his horse back out of the mire, when he heard a twig snap.

"Injuns!" he yelled, and he took off running, leaving his horse behind.

The three scouts were quickly surrounded by thirty Lenape warriors and yanked from their horses. Several warriors took off on foot after Martin. Martin ran, knowing that if he was caught, being killed was the least punishment he would get if these were Shawnee.

In the morning, the soldiers were no longer an army. Stragglers continued on their way, with Colonel Crawford and Doctor Knight leading. They had gone about two miles down the road after stopping to rest when warriors jumped out from behind trees and captured the Colonel and the doctor alive.

Colonel Crawford and Dr. Knight were brought before Hopocan. He looked them over coolly. Hopocan was bare-chested and wore only leggings, loincloth, and simple moccasins. He had a knife strapped to one side, a tomahawk on the other. He had a short grey topknot.

"You have fallen into my hands, William's son, thanks to the Great Spirit. Now, you will receive the justice you deserve," he said in English. His lips curled back, menacingly around the blue dot tattoos surrounding his mouth. He ordered the prisoners stripped, and then he personally painted their bodies with a black paint using Crawford's own shirt as a brush. "We have not forgotten what you did to my people at Gnadenhutten, William's son."

To Dr. Knight, Hopocan announced, "You will go to the Shawnee towns to see some of your old acquaintances."

Then, along with nine other prisoners, Colonel Crawford and Dr. Knight were dragged with rawhide nooses around their necks and hands tied behind them, to an old Wyandot town. Lenape Chief Wingemund led the prisoners. Chief Hopocan brought up the rear, right behind Crawford and Knight.

When the prisoners reached the outskirts of the town, the leading four prisoners were hacked to pieces with tomahawks. They were scalped, and their bloodied bodies were left sprawled on the ground. Two boys kicked around the decapitated head of an officer. The remaining five were then attacked by women and boys. Danelle joined in, hitting them with a stick. One cried out for mercy. She spat at him.

Simon Girty and several Wyandot warriors came riding up on horseback. They were all painted with war paint. They sat on their horses and watched.

"Sit. There!" Hopocan ordered Crawford. He pointed to the ground in front of a fifteen-foot high post. All around the post were burning logs. Crawford's hands were still tied behind him. A rope was attached to his wrists and fastened to the post. Men, women, and children gathered in a circle all around the burning post. Dr. Knight, with his hands tied behind him, stood and watched.

As Crawford trudged over to the high post, trying to weave around the burning logs, the rope prevented much maneuverability. Boys and women beat him with sticks and clubs. Crawford, middle-aged, friend, and business partner of George Washington, hadn't slept in two days.

Crawford knew Simon Girty well from the times they had served together at Fort Pitt.

"Girty, am I being spared the tomahawk only to be burned to death? That is a horrible way to die."

"Yes, Colonel," Girty said without emotion. "You must be burned. You must pay."

"That's a terrible way to die."

"That is their way. You murdered the Christians, and now you must pay."

"That wasn't me. I would never do that. You know that. Tell them, please. I beg you."

Hopocan raised his hands up for silence. *"This white devil has invaded our land with his army. First, he killed our praying brothers and sisters, and now he has come to kill us, too. He was a big chief, a brave soldier against people who wouldn't fight back, but now he has made the mistake of attacking warriors."*

The people yelled with approval.

"Many fathers, sons, and husbands have been killed over the years by these white liars and murderers who have invaded our land. We have every right to kill them. The Shawnee torture as a warning to other white settlers to stay away from their land. We, the Lenape, torture only when the crime is great. This is the time. We want this coward to suffer in pain as long as possible for what he has done."

Hopocan stepped back and waved his hand. Warriors stepped up all around Crawford and fired their muskets at him. They didn't use bullets but got close enough so that the exploding gunpowder sharply burned him all over his body. Then, boys stepped forward and grabbed the ends of burning sticks and stuck them in his flesh from all sides. Women, using old rags and sticks, picked up red hot coals and threw them at him. They burned as they hit him, then fell to the ground all around him. They kept throwing until there was no place for him to walk without stepping on them. He winced with each one but refused to scream his pain.

"Girty! "Crawford cried out. "I beg you! In the name of God! Shoot me!"

Girty, from horseback, held out both empty hands and laughed. "How can I? You see I have no gun."

Crawford endured the burning pokes and thrown coals for three hours before he fainted.

Finally, Hopocan stepped forward and scalped him, holding the grey, bloody locks high among cheers. Women stepped up and poured red coals on his head and body. But he wasn't dead. He stood and tried to walk but tripped and fell onto the coals. Four warriors stepped up, picked him up, and threw his body into the fire.

Girty called to Dr. Knight, "That'll be your fate, too, my friend, when you get to the Shawnee villages."

Martin thought about killing those chasing him, but being this far into the Ohio country put him at a disadvantage. He didn't even know where he was. He could easily lose them in the dark by hiding, so that's what he did. He climbed under a fallen tree and scooped leaves over himself. He heard them run past. He lay there for an hour, resting. Then, he took off running, as straight as he could, following the hilltops, all the way to the Ohio River. Once there, he dove in and   swam   across.

33 JOHN MILL'S HORSE

Lewis wasn't at the Battle of Sandusky. A friend, John Mills, was one of the survivors. After abandoning his prize stallion, he swam across the river and ran straight to the Rosencranz's cabin, where he hoped to find Lewis. Lewis was sitting out front on an upended stump while Bertha ran a comb through his long, black hair. They had been talking about money. She wanted a mirror and a new dress, and he had suggested that maybe he could set some beaver traps in the Ohio country after the army wiped out the Indians. He had seen many beavers there, especially down around the Muskingum River.

Lewis spotted Mills first. "Looks like we've got company."

Bertha looked up. "Hey, John," she called out. "Welcome back!"

Mills didn't answer, but he kept running up the hill until he reached them. He collapsed on the ground, lying flat on his back. His linen shirt was the color of dirt and was soaking wet.

"Go get him some water," Lewis ordered. Bertha hurried inside and came back with a dripping wooden cup. Mills reached up, took it, drank the whole thing in one gulp, and held it out for more.

When he cooled down and caught his breath, Mills said. "Things went bad, Lewis. Real bad. We were outnumbered, and they were angry as hornets. They chased us all the way to the river. I'm one of the lucky ones. I got away. Your brother was leading us out of there. I don't know what happened to him."

Lewis nodded. "Martin'll be alright. Don't worry about him." He remembered grandpa's charm. No Indian bullet could touch any of the Wetzel children. Lewis believed it.

"It was total confusion, Lewis. It was dark. We couldn't see where we were going, but we knew we had to get the hell out of there. A lot of guys didn't make it."

Lewis wasn't a bit surprised that they'd run into trouble. If you wanted to kill Indians, you had to outsmart them, and you couldn't do that with hundreds of noisy men tramping through the woods in broad daylight on a fine summer day.

"And I lost Twilight!"

"Oh, honey," Bertha said. She leaned down and kissed him on the forehead. "That was a beautiful horse."

"Heck of a fine horse," Lewis said. "That's too bad."

"That's why I've come," Mills said. "I know where he is. He got stuck in some mud, and I couldn't get him out. Those varmints were right on my tail. He has a bell on him, so he should be easy to find."

"What do you want of me?" Lewis' eyes opened in surprise.

"To help me get him," Mills said, getting to his feet. "Please, Lewis. That horse is too valuable to let them savages have him."

"Where did you lose him? Lewis asked.

"Can't be more than a couple of miles from the river. We were going down the creeks 'cause the Indians were watching the trails. I can lead you right there."

"Probably the injuns already have him," Lewis said matter-of-factly. "Nothing I can do."

"Please, Lewis. I'm begging you." Mill got down on his hands and knees in front of Lewis and put his palms together.

Lewis shook his head. "Those buggers are liable to scalp us both. That horse worth losing your life for?"

"Not with you along, Lewis. That's why I came straight here. You're the only one who can help me. You ain't afraid of injuns. Please! I'll give you ten Spanish dollars. Even if we don't get him back, I'll pay. What do you say, pal? Will you help me out? Here's my lucky dollar in advance. Nine more when we get back. Mills reached into the pouch at his side and pulled out the silver piece, bit on it, and handed it over to Lewis.

Lewis hefted the silver coin and flipped it in the air, catching it with one hand. He turned around and looked at Bertha.

"There's a chance they didn't find him," Mills said. "It was dark. Please! If he's gone, I'll still give you nine more dollars. I just need you along to help me stay alive in case I'm wrong. If the injuns have him, if we can't find him, we'll turn back. Deal?"

Lewis flipped the coin to Bertha. She reached for it, missed, and it went rolling along in a circle before landing with a clink.

The two crossed the river by canoe to Wheeling Island and carried the canoe to the other side and then over to Ohio's mainland. Mills led the way. The land was all hills and hollows. Lewis proceeded cautiously, darting from tree to tree with his rifle loaded and ready. Several miles from the river at the top of a hill, Mills pointed down into the ravine below. "That's the spot." It was brushy and tangled and lacked the big tree cover of the hilltops.

Lewis signaled for Mills to sit, and the two sat for a while just looking and listening.

"Could be a trap," Lewis whispered. "Be ready for anything. Stay low and don't make a sound." Rather than stand up, he pushed himself up to a squat and walked crab-like down the hill with his musket pointing the way. Mills followed behind him.

When they reached the creek bed, Mills pointed out the disturbed muck. Just then, they heard the tinkle of a bell.

"That's him. That's Twilight!" Mills whispered." He's over there." Mills pointed upstream.

Lewis didn't answer but signaled for Mills to proceed up the side of the creek where there was a deer trail. Mills started down the trail.

Knotche set the bell down on the ground and motioned for his four warriors to duck behind the bushes. They hadn't gotten more than a glimpse of the two white men. But Black Snake saw the bun of black hair tied at Lewis' neck and immediately recognized him.

He whispered, *"It's the boy* . . . but before he could finish, Carrot-top and Cockalalaman, two Lenape warriors with them, both pulled their triggers. There was a loud BOOM. And, again, BOOM. They both dropped their muskets and ran towards Mills.

Mills yelped. He'd taken a bullet in the thigh.

Knotche gave a fierce war cry and ran through the bushes towards Mills with his tomahawk drawn, right behind Cockalalaman. Carrot-top led the way. Lewis, un-hit, jumped behind a tree, spotted one of the attackers, and shot the one leading the way. He hit Carrot-top, smack in the heart. Alerted to where he was, Black Snake and Goose ran at Lewis. Black Snake carried his new musket in his right hand, loaded and ready.

Lewis called over to Mills, who was just a few feet away. "Toss me your musket. Quick!" Lewis stooped down and slid his now empty musket to Mills, pulled out his tomahawk, and tossed it over, too. "Sell your life dearly, John."

Mills flung his loaded musket to Lewis. Lewis caught it in one hand and in the same motion, dropped to one knee, aimed, and shot Cockalalaman in the forehead.

Lewis spun around and, with a yell, took off running back up the hill, trying to lead the warriors away from Mills. Knotche ran at Mills swinging his tomahawk. Mills tried to fend off the attack with Lewis' rifle, holding it up with both hands, blocking the blow. He didn't see the knife in Knotche's other hand until it was too late.

Lewis was surprised that only two attackers chased him. He wasn't sure how many there were but had expected to draw all of them away from the wounded Mills. He loaded as he ran, but he had enough confidence in his own running ability that he figured he could easily outdistance the pursuers. He dumped powder, too much powder, from the horn around his neck down into the barrel, but he didn't have time to get the bullet in, too, before Black Snake was right behind him. Lewis stopped and turned as if to shoot, and Black Snake jumped behind a big oak. Lewis took off running again and spit a bullet down the barrel. A bullet went zinging by his ear. Black Snake dropped his now unloaded new musket and took off after Lewis with a tomahawk in one hand. He gained on Lewis. Goose lagged behind. After scalping Mills, Knotche joined the pursuit.

Black Snake swung the tomahawk on a downward arc towards Lewis' head. Lewis abruptly spun around. Black Snake's wrist hit Lewis' shoulder, and his tomahawk went flying.

Lewis shoved the barrel of Mill's musket into Black Snake's belly. Black Snake grabbed the barrel with his free hand, pushing it aside, grabbed his knife from the sheath, and sliced at Wetzel's face, nicking him across one cheek.

At the same instant, Lewis jumped back out of the way of the knife, still holding on tight to the musket. Black Snake was pulled off balance, and his arm was extended, just enough for Lewis to shove the gun back into Black Snake's belly and pull the trigger. The overcharge of powder blew a hole in Black Snake's belly the size of a fist.

Lewis was running on adrenalin now. He reached down and grabbed his knife in one hand and grabbed Black Snake's mohawk hair with the other, still holding Mills' musket in it. He whacked at the scalp when he heard approaching, running footsteps.

Knotche and Goose both screamed war cries as they ran at Lewis, Knotche with his tomahawk upraised. Lewis dropped the scalp and knife and with the empty musket still in his hand, he took off running. Goose stopped, aimed, and fired just as Lewis darted behind a tree. The bullet zinged through the air and took off a piece of bark.

Lewis reached the top of the hill and kept running down the other side, spilling powder into the barrel as he went. The hill was steep. He jumped down onto a ledge of boulders and ducked behind a big rock.

The two warriors went running around the ledge, and Lewis ran to the other side. He had a perfect shot at the two and reached for a bullet. He'd already used all the bullets in his mouth, his bullet pouch empty, too. The bullets in his pouch had bounced out and went flying when he jumped, only he hadn't noticed.

He figured that Mills hadn't made it, or those two wouldn't have come after him. Without any bullets and outnumbered two to one, he weighed his options in a split second. He climbed back up the hill and ran all the way to the river. He hid Mill's musket in some weeds and swam across to Wheeling.

34 FORT HENRY

After the Indian victory at Sandusky and the ritualistic torturing of the American commander Colonel Crawford, the British urged continued Indian attacks. A large force was organized with one-hundred and fifty British Rangers and a number of warriors from various tribes who were still arriving to help fight off the invasion by Crawford's militia army. The Mohawk Joseph Brant arrived with a small contingent of Mohawk warriors. He was well received after word had spread about his victory over Colonel Lochry. The Half King Dunquat and Chief Hopocan agreed to lead the Shawnee, Lenape, Mingo, Wyandot, Miami, Ottawa, Ojibway, and Pottawatomi. Simon Girty, his brother George, Alexander McKee, and Mathew Elliot all came as advisors. They set out to attack Fort Henry after sending out scouts to reconnoiter.

On the way to Wheeling, they were met by messengers with news that General George Rogers Clark, the feared Long Knife general, was preparing to invade the Shawnee towns. The attack on Fort Henry was modified. One force, led by British Captain William Caldwell, with the assistance of Simon Girty, Mathew Elliot, and Alexander McKee, would lead fifty Loyalists and three-hundred Ottawa and Wyandot warriors to attack the Kentucky settlements to divert General Clark's invasion. Another war party, led by Dunquat and assisted by Chiefs Brant and Hopocan and three-hundred Wyandot, Shawnee, Mingo, and Lenape warriors, would attack the Long Knife fort at Wheeling and Fort Henry, as originally planned.

Knotche and Goose, after mourning the loss of their friend Black Snake, joined Hopocan's band, hoping for a chance to kill the boy whose rifle was always loaded. They knew he lived in Wheeling. They were sad and angry and sought revenge.

Dunquat warned that Fort Henry was difficult to capture. Brant suggested that perhaps they could take the fort by surprise. Instead of attempting to lure out the soldiers as Dunquat had successfully done in the first attack on Fort Henry, perhaps they could capture the whole fort and everybody in it. Not the same way Dunquat's force had done previously, but in a similar way. Brant suggested that they arrive at night, undetected. As soon as the fort gates were opened in the morning, which they always did as the whites came out to feed their animals and fetch firewood, they would rush in through the gates. Then, they could take their time attacking the surrounding cabins. Dunquat and Hopocan agreed to the Mohawk's plan.

I just want to get my hands on that boy," Knotche said. *"He'll wish we had made a warrior out of him."*

Goose agreed. That would be their first priority. *"When we get inside that fort, we can do anything we want to him. I'm going to make him pay for what he did to Black Snake."*

The people around Wheeling had been depending upon private scouts to warn them of any attacks, rather than call up the militia after the Sandusky disaster. There were just too few eligible, capable men to use militiamen. The survivors from the Sandusky Expedition had been excused from militia duty.

Everybody was frightened. They had lost a tenth of their force in the attack on Sandusky. The settlers chipped in to attract good scouts so that they could depend upon men experienced in the Indian ways. Then they could go about their business without having to look over their shoulders. Lewis and Martin both took the job. So did their friend, John Lynn. Lynn was working as a scout watching the Mingo Trail at the river ford the second week of September when he spotted the large force of British soldiers and Indians coming down the trail. He ran as fast as he could back to Wheeling to warn the settlers to fort up before the enemy forces arrived.

"They should be here any minute. They're not far behind," Lynn warned.

The Wetzels had already taken up quarters in the fort after the Sandusky fiasco. Pa and Uncle Lewis were certain there would be a follow-up to the Indian victory. With Lynn's warning, they readied for an immediate attack, but no attack came. Many thought Lynn was seeing things and just being too jumpy.

The British and Indian forces crossed the river after nightfall as planned and spread out around the fort, not realizing they had been spotted. Many of them hid in a pawpaw patch near the fort.

When the palisade gates opened in the morning, it opened just a few inches. Four jittery volunteers slipped through the gate, armed and ready, looking for any signs of the enemy, just in case Lynn had been right. An Indian was spotted before they'd gone a few feet, which was enough to convince them that Lynn was right. They called out to open the gate back up and scrambled back inside. Shots were fired. One of the four was hit by a bullet. The gate was shut before the Indians could rush it. Inside, there were twenty men and sixty women and children.

The British flag bearer and band leader, with drummers and fifers marching behind them, paraded down the road between the cornfields towards the fort gate, staying what they thought was out of musket range. George Girty, Simon's brother, along with the Wyandot warrior Goose, rode up. Goose fired his musket at the fort. Girty called out in English, "Surrender or die!"

Colonel Silas Zane, who was the senior officer inside the fort at the time, called out to the twenty men inside the fort manning the loopholes. "Give 'em our answer, boys!"

Martin and Lewis, both excellent marksmen, as well as several others, were standing on platforms inside the palisade next to the gate looking through the loopholes. Other men were scattered around at various other spots. Twenty shots rang out, putting several holes in the Union Jack.

Girty and Goose immediately turned their horses and galloped further back. Startled, thinking they were out of musket range, the bandleader quickly called out, "About face!" The British drummers and fifers wheeled and marched briskly away.

Dunquat lowered his upraised hand, and hundreds of shots rang out amid war cries and shouting. As bullets flew, the warriors rushed the fort.

Lewis killed a warrior on his first shot. So did Martin. Other attackers, too, fell. Lewis and Martin weren't the only expert riflemen. So were Hamilton Kerr and

Samuel Tomlinson. The women reloaded guns and passed them forward.

Colonel Ebenezer Zane, Silas' brother, who, along with half a dozen others, was standing at a rifle loophole in the nearby Zane family blockhouse, also fired with good effect. He rarely missed.

Silas Zane, commanding the fort, ordered the fort's new cannon be fired. The cannonballs didn't hit anybody, but the loud noise and the fiery red ball flying at the British soldiers and their Indian allies, aimed head high, scared them all as the cannonballs went careening through the cornstalks. The red-coated British soldiers and Indians scattered while the sharpshooters inside the fort fired with deadly accuracy.

Everything was quiet for most of the day. Then, the Indians rushed the fort again. Again, they were driven back by cannon fire and the sharpshooters inside the fort. The women melted lead to make more bullets. Nobody had thought of until now that most of the ammunition was being stored in the blockhouse.

At dark, it got quiet again. In Zane's blockhouse just outside the fort, Ebenezer Zane's old slave Sam spotted an Indian just outside the blockhouse with a lighted torch trying to set the building on fire. Sam shot him.

At first light, an unexpected arrival pulled ashore. A flatboat was coming downriver from Fort Pitt with a load of cannonballs, headed farther down to Fort Nelson at the Falls of the Ohio in Kentucky. The crew had stopped to take a break at Wheeling. As the crew tied up the boat, one man hopped ashore and walked up towards the fort, unaware of the ongoing attack.

The Indian attackers saw him and ran towards him, shooting, yelling, and waving tomahawks. He bolted towards the fort, the gate cracked open for him, and he made it in, slightly wounded. His crew jumped overboard and swam out into the river. The British Rangers and the Indians took control of the boat and its load of cannonballs.

It seemed like a good idea to fight cannon with cannon, and now that the British and their Indian allies had a supply of cannonballs, they were optimistic. The attackers figured they could bust down the palisades with cannonballs and rush the fort now. All they needed was a cannon. Putting the expert canoe makers to work using British ingenuity, the Wyandot warriors hollowed out a tree in no time, and they whittled it down so that it was the perfect size for a cannonball. They smoothed it out, rubbing sand inside the barrel.

The British Rangers supplied a chain to wrap around it to help make it stronger. They aimed in straight at the gate of the fort, primed it with gun powder, pushed a cannonball down into the barrel, and lit it. It didn't go as planned. The log blew up, and pieces of chain went flying in all directions, killing or maiming everyone around it.

Dunquat ordered his forces to rush the fort again. The men in the fort and the blockhouse fired back, and the Indians once again had to retreat. But gunpowder was running low in the fort.

Silas Zane asked for a volunteer to go to the blockhouse for more gunpowder. They wouldn't be able to fight off another charge without more powder. None of the Wetzels volunteered, but several other men did.

Betty Zane, Silas' and Ebenezer's younger sister, said, "If one of you should go and not make it, we'll be in trouble. We need all you fighting men. I'll go." She was sixteen, active, and athletic.

It was agreed.

The gate was opened, and she boldly walked out.

All the Indians saw her. Dunquat said to Hopocan. *"It's only a woman."* Hopocan nodded.

Goose said to Knotche. *"What's she doing?"*

"She's looking for a man. Maybe you. She would take your mind off Danelle. You might like white women."

Goose rolled his eyes and laughed. *"We should kill her before she breeds."*

Knotche, happily married, replied, *"I don't shoot women. I love them."*

Betty Zane reached the blockhouse without a shot being fired. Sam opened the door for her, and she darted in, nearly white with fright. She told her brother why she'd come. Ebenezer tied a red and white tablecloth around her waist, uncorked a powder barrel, and poured the contents into it. She held the ends of the tablecloth to her sides and ran back towards the fort.

"She runs like a frightened rabbit," Goose remarked.

Knotche immediately grasped what was going on. *"Stop her!"* He called out. Several shots rang out. The girl leaped through the air like a deer. The fort gate opened slightly, and before any shots could stop her, she darted back in, untouched.

The attackers lay siege to the fort one more day before one of their scouts reported that a company of soldiers was spotted coming their way. Dunquat, Hopocan, and Brant discussed this new event and made a decision. Most of their force would slip back across the river in order to save lives and resources. They could attack on another day. Warriors were sent out to destroy any cabins they could find.

35 DEALING WITH THE INDIANS

General Washington kept drilling his soldiers, but after Cornwallis surrendered his army at Yorktown, there were no more offensives by either side in the east. In the west, the British continued to supply muskets, bullets, and gunpowder and encouraged the natives to continue raiding the settlements. Lewis Wetzel continued to cross the river, hunting Indians. When winter came, the fighting ceased.

The two old friends had been fighting for their land and way of life for years. Knotche spent the winter playing with his baby daughter and enjoying the comforts of married life. Goose, who had never been excited about going to war after the trauma of watching his cousin Heron being killed, was starting to believe that he needed to change. He hadn't gotten what he wanted most, Danelle. He rode to Fort Detroit with a bundle of furs to sell, some of which had been Black Snake's that he hadn't sold. He had vague plans to stick around and learn English. No matter which side won in the Revolutionary War, Goose figured he was going to have to live with either the English or the Americans. No matter how many battles the natives won, there were always more settlers.

The British and the Americans knew peace negotiations were going on in Paris, and they waited impatiently. Washington had his hands full with an officers' rebellion at Newburgh. Many of his officers had lost their homes and fortunes during the war, while much of the rest of the country had prospered. They believed the country owed them something for their commitment to serve, and they were worried that they would be dismissed without the pay owed them, as well as the land bounties promised for serving until the war's end.

Washington was ordered to make plans to disband the army.

Rumors began floating around that a peace treaty had been reached.

More rumors started floating around that the army would refuse to disband until they were paid. Or that they would take their guns and move to the unsettled country far away from an ungrateful population. Soldiers marched on Philadelphia and blocked the Continental Congress from leaving the State House, where they were meeting. The soldiers refused to let the delegates leave until they were paid. Congress fled in the night and reconvened across the river in Princeton, New Jersey.

The Continental Congress was not in session when the approved Treaty of Paris ending the war finally arrived on American shores. It had taken nearly two months to arrive by sailing ship. No Indians were present or represented at the treaty. Not from the Iroquois, not from the Wyandot, not from the Ottawa, not from the Lenape, not from the Shawnee. None of the native issues had been resolved.

The Indians kept up their raids.

There was a six-month deadline to exchange ratifications on the Treaty, so there wasn't a lot of time to debate the Treaty and return it to Paris. But for the next month and a half, not enough delegates attended the Congressional sessions to provide a quorum of seven states, much less the nine needed to ratify the Treaty.

In January of '84, barely two months before the ratification deadline, and with time running out to get a signed treaty back to Paris on a sailing ship, the new President of the Continental Congress, Thomas Mifflin, in desperation, sent his private secretary, Josiah Harmar, to try to round up the required delegates to ratify the treaty.

Lt. Colonel Josiah Harmar, from Pennsylvania, had served with General Nathaniel Greene as his Adjutant General in the southern campaign. He was on the list of gentlemen personally known by General Washington as some of the best Continental officers in the army. Mifflin sent Harmar to round up the New Jersey and Connecticut delegates and try to bring back the South Carolina delegate, too, who was sick in Philadelphia.

Harmar traveled by horse and stagecoach and made it back with the needed delegates nine days later. The next day, the Treaty was ratified.

Harmar, having proved that he could get things done, was then immediately given the task of delivering the signed and ratified Treaty to the new country's representative in Paris. A duplicate and a triplicate of the Treaty were given to other couriers to ensure delivery. Funds were short even to pay for Harmar's trip. He was given enough money for a one-way ticket. He was expected to find his own way back home. He ended up borrowing money from General Lafayette while in Europe and riding back home with Lafayette on Lafayette's own ship.

The army was dismissed. The American Finance Minister, Robert Morris, a wealthy man, announced, "I will never be the Minister of Injustice," and wrote personal checks to the soldiers for three months' pay. But many of the soldiers sold the checks at a large discount, especially those in far off places like Fort Pitt, so they would have the money to get home.

Unfortunately for Morris, who had made his fortune in the shipping business, the British clamped down on all American shipping after its loss at Yorktown. Most of Morris' ships and their cargo were confiscated, and he ended up in debtor's prison.

Those officers and soldiers who qualified for pensions and land bounties by serving until the end of the war were sent home with a paper pension. George Washington was not happy with the situation. He thought his troops, the ones who had honorably served to the very end while their peers who had not served had prospered, were "disbanded like a set of beggars - needy, distressed and without prospects."

The Treaty of Paris officially ended the Revolutionary War. Great Britain recognized the American states as an independent, sovereign country and ceded land to the new United States of America west all the way to the Mississippi River, which was the border of Spanish territory.

In Treaty negotiations, the British agreed to give up the forts along the border separating Canada from the American states, though they were reluctant to give up the lucrative fur trade with the Indians that these forts supported. Congress ordered all troops discharged by June 2, 1784, except twenty-five soldiers to guard the supplies at Fort Pitt and another fifty-five at West Point.

According to Congress, "Standing armies in time of peace are inconsistent with the principles of republican government, dangerous to the liberties of free people and generally converted into destructive engines for establishing despotism."

The Iroquois and the western tribes, the Lenape, Shawnee, Wyandot, Ottawa, and the other Ohio valley tribes, allies of the British, did not believe they had been defeated. They had just wiped out an attacking American army and had burned alive its leader, Colonel William Crawford. They considered much of the land the British ceded to the Americans as belonging to them, not the British. The British had no right to cede their land.

The reduction of the Continental force in the west left only the militia to fight the Indians, who were still attacking settlements. Former Continental General Henry Knox was appointed Secretary of War. He was now the top official overseeing the military. Knox wrote to Washington asking for his advice about manning the western forts. How could he do it with militia and only twenty-five Continentals? They were both aware of the problems with the militia. Knox wrote Washington that the militia would "defeat the purposes by their own imbecility." Washington, who was glad to be home in Mount Vernon, offered his advice: the country needs more soldiers.

The year after the treaty was signed, twenty-thousand immigrants floated down the Ohio River past the Muskingum River to the Kentuck lands. Most of the newcomers were British from the north of England, Scotland, and Northern Ireland. There were large numbers of Germans, too, including Hessian mercenaries brought over to fight the Americans.

Battles raged back and forth across the Ohio River, particularly in Virginia's western portion called by the Shawnee the Kentuck. The native tribes hadn't stopped fighting. They didn't even see how the Treaty of Paris applied to them. They hadn't agreed to anything. The Shawnee raided the Kentuck settlements, and the Kentuckians responded by raiding the Shawnee villages. Other tribes, including the Miami, the Pottawatomie, and the Lenape, continued to fight the intruders elsewhere, believing that any plunder was rightfully theirs since the trespassers had no right to even be on native land.

Knotche and Goose continued going on raiding parties as called for by their leaders in order to protect their land, their way of living, and their lives. But for every cabin they burned, two more would take its place. Most of the Indians were a warrior people, but they weren't equipped, nor did their lifestyle permit being at war for years without end.

At Knox's request, following Washington's advice, Congress called on several states including Connecticut, New York, New Jersey, and Pennsylvania to supply troops not only to protect the settlers on the western frontier but to keep squatters from taking over the newly ceded western land before it could be surveyed. They planned to give out the promised land bounties and put the rest of the land up for sale to help pay the country's war debt. Eight companies of infantry and two companies of artillery were deemed sufficient for the American army, nearly all of it on the frontier.

Josiah Harmar, President Mifflin's private secretary and the messenger who had delivered the Treaty to Paris, was appointed the new Commander of the American forces. Lieutenant Colonel Harmar made his headquarters at Fort McIntosh, the fort built by General Lachlan McIntosh near where Chief White Eyes had been murdered. Harmar found squatters had built cabins and cleared land at nearly every tributary of the Ohio River. In the larger valleys like the Muskingum and the Hockhocking, settlements of up to three-hundred families had sprung up. Many immigrants saw the American forts on the Indian side of the river as an invitation to live on that land and be protected by American soldiers. Harmar sent out squads up and down the Ohio River, all the way to the French villages near Vincennes to burn down squatters' cabins.

Harmar's task of keeping the squatters off the newly ceded land and protecting settlers on the other side of the river was nearly impossible. He had taken over the task formerly assigned to the Commandant of the Western District to protect settlers along twelve-hundred miles of borderland, with the added task now of keeping out squatters. At the same time, the British, who had not relinquished its forts along the northern border as agreed to in the Treaty of Paris, continued to supply the Indians with muskets and ammunition and encouraged them to continue their attacks. A constant struggle continued between bands of Indians on the one side of the Ohio River and border settlers on the other as they raided each other, back and forth.

Knox recommended that peace be made with the Indians. It was too expensive to fight them. They were too formidable an enemy, with fifteen-hundred to two-thousand armed warriors. He had less than six-hundred soldiers on the frontier and had difficulty recruiting more. Harmar had to keep sending his officers back east on recruiting missions just to replace the incorrigible soldiers and deserters he was able to enlist for the low pay, dangerous assignments, and primitive living conditions.

Knox discussed the situation with Washington. The two leaders were sympathetic to the plight of the Indians and believed, like most intelligent, educated people of the time, that the natives should be induced to abandon the primitive hunting and gathering ways they were accustomed to and join the modern world. Their thinking was that the Indians didn't need all that rich land. The growing country did. The country's borders needed to be protected. Now, enemies surrounded the United States. The British to the north, the Spanish to the south and west, and Indians everywhere. There was no question in leadership circles that since the Indians had supported the British cause, they had forfeited their territory. No thought was given to the murders of Chief White Eyes and Chief Cornstalk at American hands that drove the Lenape and Shawnee to the British. The question facing American leaders was how to get the Indians to stop fighting and allow peaceful settlement on Indian land?

The Indians had their own dilemma. How could they stop the ever-increasing number of foreigners who were trying to kill them, destroy their way of life, and take the land handed down to them by their forefathers?

A year after the Treaty of Paris, a second Treaty of Fort Stanwix was held. In the first Treaty of Fort Stanwix, the Iroquois Nation had sold the land bordering the Ohio Country to the British, land they claimed by conquest in the Beaver Wars a hundred years before, but which was occupied by others, including the Wyandot, Lenape, and Shawnee. That was the treaty that had attracted the Wetzels, the Bonnetts, the Zanes, and many others. The second Fort Stanwix Treaty was similar to the first, only this time the land in question was across the Ohio River in the Ohio valley. This was the land of the Lenape, Wyandot, and Shawnee. The Mohawk Joseph Brant was the lead negotiator for the Iroquois Nation, and he began the negotiations by telling the American commissioners that "we are sent to make peace and that we are not authorized to stipulate any particular cessions of land."

The Americans' negotiators claimed that the Iroquois had forfeited their right to the land by allying with the British. Brant left the negotiations early for a planned trip to England. Although Seneca Chief Cornplanter signed the treaty, the Six Nations of the Iroquois Council refused to ratify the Treaty of Fort Stanwix because their delegates didn't have the authority to sell such a large tract of land – much of the Ohio country.

Just after the Treaty was signed, physician and diplomat Arthur Lee, one of the commissioners representing the American interests and not fond of any natives, wrote President Mifflin about the Iroquois, who were now living in Canada. "They are animals that need to be subdued . . . or they will be mischievous, and fear alone will affect their submission, these savages who will be obliged to retire to the interior like their kindred wolves."

The western tribes who lived on the land, just as in the first Fort Stanwix Treaty, weren't invited to participate in the treaty. They refused to accept the sale of their land by the Iroquois. So another treaty was held the following year at Fort McIntosh with the Wyandot, the Lenape, Chippewa, and Ottawa. Two of the same commissioners, General Richard Butler and Arthur Lee, were joined by General George Rogers Clark. The commissioners ordered that a proclamation be posted while negotiations were underway that all western land was closed to occupation. In other words - squatters stay out - until it was surveyed and put up for sale.

Selling of land by Indians wasn't a new concept. With tribal consent, land was occasionally given or sold to others. But for this treaty, Hopocan and the other leaders were plied with whiskey and gifts and told to sign this treaty, not understanding the importance of the X's they made on paper or what the treaty was all about.

Both Knotche and Goose attended the treaty. Fort McIntosh was just a couple of days' travel from their lake village. Hopocan had asked them to come and to participate in the festivities. The idea that the Indian leaders were agreeing to give away the land they lived and hunted on never occurred to them. They thought it was just a friendly gathering agreeing to end the conflict. The Americans fed them and gave them gifts of blankets, and hung medallions around their necks with bright red ribbons. This treaty took the land of southern and eastern Ohio, east of the Cuyahoga and Muskingum Rivers. No payment was offered or given.

36 MORE TREATIES

The Shawnee and their relatives, the Miami, refused to accept the cession of any of the Ohio land. The Shawnee kept attacking and looting boats coming down the Ohio River and capturing or killing trespassers who tried to fight their way past them. They continued to use captives to lure boaters to shore.

Shawnee scouts reported a new activity in the Kentuck land. The militia started mustering for duty armed and in flotillas. The Shawnee War Chief Blue Jacket sent a small band to spy on them and report daily. The Lenape reported similar activity at Fort Pitt. The Shawnee continued sending bands of warriors to stop the immigrants from coming downriver, but there was such a flood that their forces had little effect. It was like piling sand in a roaring river to stop the flow.

The following year, a Treaty was held with the Shawnee, led by ninety-four-year-old Chief Moluntha, who had taken over leadership of the Shawnee after the murder of Chief Cornstalk at Fort Randolph several years before. The Shawnee met the commissioners, Generals Richard Butler and George Rogers Clark, at the new Fort Finney, a fort built a few months before at the Great Miami River's mouth near Cincinnati on Shawnee land. The commissioners told the Shawnee chiefs that they were not free to live wherever they wanted but would live where the commissioners stipulated.

Tame Hawk, a Shawnee war chief called Captain Johnny by the whites, said, *"We do not understand measuring out the lands. It is all ours!"*

Butler, who was shortly after appointed the Superintendent of Indian Affairs, told the chiefs through his translator, *"We plainly tell you this country belongs to the United States. Their blood hath defended it and will forever protect it."*

The Shawnee gave their answer to taking their land and telling them they were limited to living on a reservation. Moluntha, walking tall and proud as old as he was, shuffled up to the commissioners and presented them a black belt of wampum. War!

General Clark swept the black wampum belt from the table onto the ground and stomped on it. Clark had a reputation among the Indians for being a fierce and effective warrior chief. He glared at Moluntha. The translator said, *"Refuse to accept the treaty, and there will be war. We have more soldiers than there are stars in the sky, and we will kill every Shawnee man, woman, and child."*

The negotiations broke up. The next day, some of the Shawnee chiefs, including Moluntha, signed the treaty. Others left in disgust, refusing to sign. There was no payment offered for the land.

Three months later, Moluntha and two others, The Shade and Red Pole, met with the British. They told the British officials, *"We have never been in more need of your friendship and good offices. We have been cheated on by the Americans who are still striving to work our destruction, and without your assistance, they may be able to accomplish their ends."*

Later that year, Colonel Harmar heard a rumor from spies living near the Miami Indians, who lived in the northwest corner of the Ohio country. The intelligence report stated that General George Rogers Clark had been authorized by the state of Virginia to attack the Miami. Harmar reported that news to Knox. Was the federal government in charge in the Northwest Territory, or states like Virginia, he wanted to know?

The Shawnee also heard of the upcoming expedition of an attack on the Miami towns. The Miami and Shawnee were relatives. Shawnee warriors left their own towns undefended and went north to help their Miami kinsmen defend their homes.

General Clark, though, couldn't raise enough militiamen for the campaign he planned. He did manage to muster enough militiamen to direct a raid on the undefended Shawnee towns, however. His militiamen burned thirteen Shawnee towns, killing old men, women, and children and taking scalps and prisoners. One of the towns they destroyed was the old Shawnee Chief Moluntha's home. Moluntha was too feeble to travel with his warriors north to Miami country. He surrendered to the militia troops. Disobeying orders to the contrary, a militiaman whacked Moluntha in the head with an axe.

37 DISASTER FOR THE WETZELS

Lewis told his Pa that in his explorations he had seen that the Muskingum River was "plum full of beaver". But Lewis didn't like hanging around there. It was too dangerous, especially in the winter. His tracks were too easy to follow.

With the various peace treaties with the Indians, Pa figured it was a good time to go beaver hunting down on the Muskingum before everybody else got the idea. If they were as thick as Lewis said, they could make a good payday. With his sons George and Lewis, and his friend Miller, in Miller's canoe, the four paddled downriver. Miller's dog stood with his front legs on the bow.

Just before heading downriver, they had seen a small sailing ship from the Monongahela River loaded with flour. It had stopped briefly at Wheeling on its maiden attempt to tap into the higher prices at the New Orleans market.

After leaving Wheeling, the ship, commanded by Joseph Parkinson, ran aground on a sandbar jutting out from Captina Island. The fog had been thick, and neither the captain nor the lookouts had seen the island until too late. They tried to steer around it, but the wind was light and the current too strong. The crew spent the day unloading the cargo in order to lighten the load. It was dark by the time they were able to row the anchor out and kedge the ship off the sandbar. Instead of proceeding, the Captain decided to anchor for the night and proceed in the morning.

A Shawnee river raiding party had been watching them. Just before dawn, the warriors paddled out and hid just below the bow. Some of the warriors were for climbing aboard and attacking the crew members sleeping below decks. But the vessel was something that they'd never seen before, and the Shawnee feared a trap. They decided to wait until someone showed themselves. It shouldn't be long before the sun rose. The plan was to shoot the first man coming out of the hatch, then, with the hatch open, they could attack.

It didn't quite go as planned. Two men came out on the deck together. They were both shot.

Eighteen-year-old Tecumseh, Standing Tree's young friend, was the first on deck and rushed the open hatchway. Seeing the difficulty of trying to rush below decks down a ladder, he called out in his broken English, "Surrender! No kill!"

One by one, the sailors ascended the ladder with their arms held up. Eleven of them. The Shawnee war party was thirty. The prisoners were assembled on shore, where the Shawnee planned to march them to Fort Detroit for a reward. They were still unloading the flour bags and piling them into their canoes when the Wetzel's canoe came around the corner.

The Wetzels had just put Miller ashore a few minutes before when he had spotted an elk.

Warriors immediately shot at the canoe. George was hit in the chest. Miller, hearing the shots, came running up and saw the Shawnee shooting at the canoe. He fired, hit one warrior, and then took off running away from them.

George yelled, "Duck! I'm a dead man. I'll get us away." He dug his paddle deep and headed for the island. Blood spurted from the hole in his chest. The bullet that hit him also killed Miller's dog. Pa, too, was hit by a bullet and slumped down in the canoe. Lewis returned fire, then ducked down, reloading as fast as he could. He shot, reloaded, and shot again. The Shawnee didn't pursue.

When he saw the canoe paddling towards the Virginia shore, Miller dove in the river and swam across. He helped Lewis carry George ashore and lay him down. Blood was squirting from his chest with each breath. He died just before dark. Pa was already dead from a bullet in the forehead. They buried them both.

"I'm going to make those buggers pay," Lewis declared. "You'll see! They'll wish they never fooled with Lewis Wetzel!" He was up early, but the Shawnee were gone.

Mary Wetzel wouldn't speak to anyone for a month. Her hair went from black to white overnight. She spent all her days working in the garden, planting every kind of vegetable seed she could get ahold of, and flowers, too. Eva took over all the household chores.

A private funeral service was held at the Wetzel cabin. It wasn't safe to go to Captina Island, where the two Wetzels had been hastily buried. Lewis Wetzel, the most famous Indian killer on the frontier, was in shock. He moped around day after day, swearing revenge. He stared across the river, but couldn't or wouldn't act as summer turned into fall and the leaves started changing color and then falling. And still, he didn't act. It was like magma building up inside a mountain, and when it burst, there would be hell to pay.

APPENDIX

Black Snake - fictional Mingo warrior

Brady, Sam-a famous Irish-American scout and Revolutionary War Officer; Born1756 in Shippensburg, PA, Died 1795 Short Creek, W. VA

Brant, Joseph aka Thayendanegea - Mohawk military and political leader who fought for the British during the Revolutionary War; Born 1743 Ohio Country, Died 1807 Upper Canada

Brodhead, Daniel IV- American Military leader during the Revolutionary War; Born Marbletown, NY, 1736; Died Milford, PA 1809

Buckongahelas - Lenape chief and warrior; Born 1720, Died 1804 Indiana

Clark, George Rogers - successful Kentucky militia-leader during Revolutionary War; highest ranking militia officer; born Albemarle County, VA in 1752, Died 1818 in Louisville, KY

Continentals - the army created by the 2nd Continental Congress after the outbreak of the Revolutionary War. Soldiers from all 13 colonies and led by General George Washington

Cornstalk - aka Holokeska - B. 1720 in Penn; Died Nov 10, 1777; Shawnee chief who led the Shawnee during Lord Dunmore's War; murdered while under house arrest at Ft. Randolph

Crawford, Col. William - American soldier, surveyor of George Washington's land and his real estate agent; B. 1732 in Spotsylvania County, PA, died 1782, Sandusky River, OH

Depeyster, Arent - former British officer during the French and Indian War; Commandant of Fort Detroit; replaced Lt Governor Henry Hamilton directing Indian attacks after Hamilton's capture; B.1736 in New York, D.1822 Dumfries, United Kingdom.

fire-cake - flour and water cooked over a fire

Dunquat - aka Petawontakas and Pomoacan - Wyandot leader and Half King; B. 1740; D- uncertain.

Fort Henry - American fort at Wheeling, W. VA. built by the order of British Royal Governor of Virginia in 1774 and renamed Fort Henry to honor Patrick Henry, Revolutionary Governor of Virginia, when the Revolutionary War broke out.

Fort Laurens - American Fort built 1778 in NE Ohio by General Lachlan McIntosh, named for Henry Laurens, President of the Continental Congress

Fort McIntosh - American fort built at the confluence of the Ohio and Beaver Rivers in PA, 1778

Fort Pitt - built by the British during the French and Indian War at the confluence of the Monongahela and Allegheny Rivers which forms the Ohio River. Built near the site of the French Fort Duquesne. After Pontiac's Rebellion, it was taken over by Virginia and renamed Fort Dunmore. During the Revolutionary War, it became the headquarters for the Continental Army's Western District

Fort Randolph - American fort built at the confluence of the Ohio and Kanawha Rivers, W. VA., 1776

Fort Stanwix - built by the British in central New York. Two important treaties were conducted there. In the first, the Iroquois Nation sold to the British land bordering the Ohio River in Virginia; in the second, the Iroquois sold land to the Americans in the Ohio country

Ganyo gowa - A Lenape character meaning great game; an animal with special powers believed to be the leader of other animals

Gibson, Colonel John B. 1740, Penn; D. 1822; Veteran of French & Indian War, Lord Dunmore's War, Revolutionary War; Indian trader captured by Lenape during Pontiac's Rebellion and condemned to be burned. Escaped death when adopted by a woman whose son was killed; married Koonay, a relative of the Mingo leader Logan. Pregnant Koonay was murdered by the Greathouse brothers, and the baby was cut from her belly and bashed against a tree during the Yellow Creek massacre; commanded Fort Laurens during the winter 1778-9; Commanded Ft. Pitt after Colonel Brodhead was removed.

Girty, Simon - born 1741 Pennsylvania, Died blind in 1818; he and his 4 brothers were captured by the Lenape during the French and Indian War. His father, an Irish immigrant and trader, was killed in a duel. His stepfather was ritualistically killed by the Lenape. His mother, brother James, 13, and young step-brother John were raised by the Shawnee. Brother George, 10, was raised by the Lenape. Simon, at 11, was adopted by Guyasuta, a Seneca and Half King. Simon was returned to his family at the end of Pontiac's Rebellion. He remained sympathetic to the Indians. He had learned 11 languages during his captivity and was the principal interpreter during the Fort Stanwix Treaty and scout and interpreter for Lord Dunmore during Lord Dunmore's War

Glickican - aka Isaac - lay leader of the Moravian church murdered in the Gnadenhutten massacre. Former war chief of the Lenape during the French and Indian War

Gnadenhutten - Pronounced juh-nay-tin-hut-in; German for "log tabernacle"; the 2nd Moravian Lenape village, built in 1772

Goose - fictional Wyandot warriors

Greathouse brothers- Daniel B.1750 D. 1775 of measles; Jacob B. 1752 D. 1777 killed during Foreman's massacre; along with 20 other frontiersmen, they attacked and killed the Mingo family of James Logan, who was friendly with the settlers. No one was brought to justice, but they didn't live long. Logan's consequent revenge resulted in Lord Dunmore's War against the Shawnee

Half King - the term used by the British to describe the Iroquois emissary who administered the Ohio country land on the Iroquois' behalf. It was the Half King Tanacharison who, along with George Washington, started the French and Indian War.

Hamilton, Henry B. 1734 in Ireland, D. 1796; Lt. Governor of British Canada, Superintendent of Indian Affairs and British commander of Fort Detroit; known as the "hair buyer" for paying Indian allies for scalps; captured by General George Rogers Clark and imprisoned in Virginia until released in a prisoner exchange

Hand, Edward - Born 1744 in Ireland, Died 1802, PA. Continental General, Commander of Ft Pitt; led the Squaw Campaign, participated in Sullivan's raid on the Iroquois and Battle of Yorktown

Heckewelder, John - B.1743 in England, D.1823 PA, Missionary for the Moravian Church and spy for the Americans

Heron - fictional Wyandot warrior

Hillbilly - a term that developed for followers of King William of Orange for Scottish and Irish immigrants who fled to America and lived in the Appalachian Mountains

Hopocan- is a translation for the other nickname, Pipe. Lenape war chief, native name Konieschquanoheel (Maker of Daylight). Born 1725, Died -date unclear 1793 or 1818.

Confusion is probably a result of his son also going by the name Capt. Pipe.

Huron- Northern-Iroquoian speaking tribe that ranged from Lake Ontario to Georgian Bay; primarily farmers, supplementing food with hunting and fishing; lived in long houses; the Huron Confederacy was defeated by the Iroquois Nation. The remnants became Wyandot

Isaac - See Glickican

Kentuck- primarily hunting ground for Chickasaw, Cherokee and Shawnee; the Shawnee lived there occasionally

Killbuck - aka Gelelemend B. 1741 Penn; D. 1811; leader of the Lenape after the death of Chief White Eyes; remained loyal to the Americans and led Col Brodhead against his own people; converted to the Moravian Church; grand-son of the Lenape Chief Netawatwees

Knight, Dr. John - army surgeon on the Sandusky Expedition; for more details, see journals.psu.edu "The Historical Accuracy of the Captivity Narrative of Doctor John Knight" by Parker B. Brown

Knotche - fictional Munsee warrior

Kuhn - aka Zhau-shoo-to; white man who became a Wyandot warrior and village chief

Land-jobber – one who makes a business of buying and selling land

Lenape - meaning "original person" indigenous people called by the British "Delaware" because of where they lived: originally New Jersey, eastern Penn, Delaware watershed, New York City, Long Island, Lower Hudson Valley; encountered first Europeans in 1524;pushed out of their homelands by expanding European colonies.

Lichtenau - the 3rd Moravian village built in the 1770's after the success of converting Lenape to Christianity by the missionaries Zeisberger and Heckewelder among others.

Logan, James - a Mingo known for retaliating against settlers after his family was brutally murdered at the Yellow Creek Massacre led by the Greathouse brothers. His retaliation helped spark Lord Dunmore's War. Afterwards, he became famous for what is called Logan's lament: "I appeal to any white man to say, if ever he entered Logan's cabin hungry, and he gave him not meat; if ever he came cold and naked, and he clothed him not. During the course of the last long and bloody war, Logan remained idle in his cabin, an advocate for peace. Such was my love for the whites, that my countrymen pointed as they passed, and said, Logan is the friend of the white men. I have even thought to live with you but for the injuries of one man. Col Cresap the last spring, in cold blood, and unprovoked, murdered all the relations of Logan, not sparing even my women and children. There runs not a drop of my blood in the veins of any living creature. This has called on me for revenge. I have sought it: I have killed many: I have fully glutted my vengeance. For my country, I rejoice at the beams of peace. But do not harbor a thought that mine is the joy of fear. Logan never felt fear. He will not turn on his heel to save his life. Who is there to mourn for Logan? Not one. (Logan was mistaken - it was not Col Cresap, but Daniel Greathouse who led the massacre)

Lochry, Colonel Archibald - B. 1733, D. 1781; a leader and large land-owner in Westmoreland County, Penn; organized militia to join General George Rogers Clark in the task of burning Indian towns and capturing Fort Detroit; his militiamen were killed or taken prisoner by George Girty and Joseph Brant, the Mohawk leader

McKee, Alexander- B. 1735, D. 1799; prominent Indian trader taught the Shawnee ways by his mother, raised and married Shawnee; deserted the American cause and joined the British becoming a leader in Indian affairs

McIntosh, General Lachlan - B. 1725 in Scotland, D. 1806; transferred from Georgia to Valley Forge after killing in a duel Button Gwinnett, an influential politician and signer of the Declaration of Independence; appointed Commander of the Western District succeeding General Edward Hand; built Fort McIntosh and For Laurens; Chief White Eyes, ally and leading chief of the Lenape, was murdered while guiding McIntosh to suitable fort sites

Mingo - the name for Seneca Indians of the Iroquois Nation living in the Ohio country

Moravian - one of the oldest Protestant denominations in the world, founded in 1457 in Bohemia

Ononharoia - literally "turning the brain upside down"; a dream sharing festival of the Iroquois and Wyandot

Shemanthe - Long Knife or Virginian

Salem - Moravian town built in 1780 in the Tuscarawa River Valley,

Senseman, Gottlob-Moravian missionary who accompanied David Zeisberger on many expeditions

Shawnee - Algonquian speaking, semi-migratory tribe primarily inhabiting the Ohio Valley.

Shoenbruen - first Christian (Moravian) village in Ohio built in 1772

Standing Tree - fictional Shawnee warrior

Transylvania - the name of the Kentucky land purchased from the Cherokee in 1775 in central and eastern Kentucky; this was historical hunting grounds of both the Cherokee and the Shawnee and had been sold by the Iroquois in the Treaty of Ft Stanwix in 1768 to the British. In 1776, the Virginia Assembly invalidated the purchase

Wehixamukes - pronounced way-heka- MOO- kase - a trickster with supernatural powers who takes things literally

White Eyes - aka Koquethagechton and George White Eyes; b. 1730 in Penn, D. Nov, 5, 1775;   Principal chief of the Lenape and ally of the Americans during the Revolutionary War; agreed to lead General McIntosh to select fort sites on Lenape land as the Americans sought to capture the British fort at Detroit; his murder was covered up and later revealed by his friend Colonel George Morgan with claims that he was killed by a militia officer.

Wingemund - a Lenape shaman

Wyandot - aka Wyandotte and Wendat; Iroquoian speaking tribe descended from the Huron living in Ohio and southern Michigan

Zeisberger, David B. 1721 in Moravia (Czech Republic), D. 1808; senior Moravian missionary who called themselves "United Brethren"; invited in 1745 to live among the Mohawk; later missionary to the Lenape; arrested and held prisoner by the British at Fort Detroit

ABOUT THE AUTHOR

Norbert Aubrey set out to find gold coins, perhaps lost by the loggers where he lives in Mendocino County, California. When the area was first settled, loggers cut the giant redwoods and were paid in gold. There were no banks. He did a little research and found that the Greenwood brothers settled in the nearby town of Elk which had formerly been called Greenwood. They were hunters, hired to feed the loggers on the plentiful elk, bear and deer. Their father, Old Greenwood, was a remnant of the Rocky Mountain fur trappers. One thing led to another, as it often does, and Norbert learned that the Rocky Mountains were opened to fur trapping by the Lewis and Clark Expedition's report that the beaver, a valuable commodity at the time, were more numerous than buffalo. When he read the Lewis and Clark accounts of the Mandan and Aricka and Blackfeet and Crow natives who had rarely even seen a white or black man, Norbert was hooked. Just a few years before the Lewis and Clark Expedition, the boundary of the settled area in the United States had been the Appalachian Mountains, where The Warriors trilogy takes place. Norbert is a graduate of Ohio University, a retired Naval Reserve Supply Officer, a meditator and martial arts practitioner. He has a son in California, another in Florida and a daughter in Ohio.

AUBREY

Made in the USA
Monee, IL
28 April 2023

32654382R00144